ALL THAT IS GOLD

ALL THAT IS GOLD

(Wanderings Part 3)

JOHN E. BEERBOWER

P.J.BEAR

CONTENTS

To Those Who Wander

"All that is gold does not glitter,
Not all those who wander are lost, ...
From the ashes a fire shall be woken,
A light from the shadows shall spring;
Renewed shall be blade that was broken,
The crownless again shall be king."

J.R.R. Tolkien
The Fellowship of the Ring

"Wanderer, your footsteps are the road,
and nothing more;
wanderer, there is no road,
the road is made by walking.
By walking one makes the road,
and upon glancing behind
one sees the path
that never will be trod again."

Antonio Machado
Campos de Castilla

Preamble

I was drawn to the quotation from J.R.R. Tolkien by the second line, which fits the theme of my series of books: Wanderings: "Not all those who wander are lost." But, the first line then attracted me:

"All that is gold does not glitter".

The converse of Shakespeare's much earlier and better known line from The Merchant of Venice: "All that glitters is not gold".

The two cautionary statements seem fitting. The flashy, catchy sentences may contain little wisdom. And, the truest sentences may seem most dull.

Again, I wrote with my eyes, all except for the chapter "My Ancestry", which is developed from something I had prepared in 2005. We recently resumed listening to Apple Music playlists again. This time 1960s rather than Classic Country. It shows in my writings. Regular purchases of Kindle books have enabled me to keep reading, now that I can no longer hold a book or turn pages. The Kindle App has also allowed me to continue to quote writings in which something is expressed more eloquently than I can manage.

Of course, much of what follows neither is gold nor glitters.

ME (AGAIN)

"It is important to tell at least from time to time
the secret of who we truly and fully are
—even if we tell it only to ourselves—
because otherwise we run the risk of losing track ...
and little by little come to accept instead
the highly edited version which we put forth."

Frederick Buechner
Telling Secrets
(1991)

I write about all this at the request of my daughter. She says she wants to know what I am/was really like. The process has given me some surprises, though. So, I think it is a good exercise.

Overwhelmed

After considerable reflection, I have realized that I spent most of my adult life on the verge of being overwhelmed. Maybe, I should say "feeling on the verge," but I generally did not "feel" it. I thought I felt fine, that I was coping well with the pressures and stress. If anyone had asked, I would have said "no problem". I was aware of no problem.

On the relatively rare occasion, only when alone, I would have a brief panic attack, convinced that I could not continue on. My refuge was to reassure myself that I could always withdraw from my accounts enough money to live on and disappear, into the woods probably. It was not a fantasy in which I indulged, but a safety valve, an escape route I kept available. Knowing it was there, I would pick up the pieces I could find and continue forward, push on. Perhaps another sign, un-recognized, came in my dreams. They were full of anxiety: I was lost, I was late, I could not find my hotel room or the meeting place, I had for-gotten that I was enrolled in a course and it was exam day, Or, I could not find my schedule or the right lecture hall. And, more of the same. Sometimes, leaving me wide awake for hours. And, a final potential, but similarly ignored, warning was my experience of sudden outbursts of anger, uncontrollable but short-lived rage. The frustrations would become unmanageable, unbearable. Then, I would recover.

But, I was fine. I could handle it all. I thought I was Superman.

Now, I was, in fact, taking on a pretty heavy load. I had a high-pressure career, with colleagues who were not all supportive. I was the primary parent of two children. I was trying to assist my wife's career. I chose to engage in continual, endless real estate projects. (Over 35 years, we owned or rented some 21 places in four different countries, 14 of which we extensively renovated. For years, we had three or four houses at a time.) Meanwhile, I served on several charity and professional boards and committees. And, I had some very traumatic marital issues. I am not going to describe the marital episodes. There was nothing that has not already been written about, frequently and well, by others, and no lessons to be shared. (Moreover, I realize that I am not actually beyond all capacity for embarrassment.)

Why did I live like that?

I have already described how the influence and encouragement of my wife helped unleash in me ambition, acquisitiveness and, even, greed. I aspired to more, much more, than the happy life of my parents. But, there was something else. During my senior year at Amherst, during the height of the protests against the Vietnam War following the invasion of Cambodia, I experienced an epiphany. The students went "on strike", as did many colleges and universities. Then, I witnessed the impotence and irrelevance of the Academy. I saw the weaknesses and helplessness —and disbelief— of many of the faculty. And, I observed the strength and wisdom of some of the Trustees. I decided to embrace the vision that I later discovered expressed in Teddy Roosevelt's speech *The Arena*. I determined, contrary to my inner nature, to try to be a participant in the "real world," not just a voyeur.

"A lot of people see doubt as a legitimate philosophical posture.
They think of themselves in the middle,
whereas, of course, really they're nowhere.
No battle was ever won by spectators, was it?"

John le Carré
The Honourable Schoolboy, p.115.

I have used this quotation from George Smiley elsewhere. That prior use was ambiguous. But, when I first read it, in my 30s, I was in complete, enthusiastic agreement. No spectators ever won a battle. Of course not. Or, did they?

Now, I am of a different view. Maybe not a battle, but the war. The silent, decent, unwilling spectators have survived; have continued to persist, to carry on their lives, with their families, their loved ones; to bear their tragedies and celebrate their joys. With tenacity, with patience, with hope, they have continued to win the war, despite the outcomes of the battles.

Yet, I do not regret overextending myself, only how I handled it emotionally.

I spent several years as hiring partner at my firm. I interviewed hundreds of applicants. Many expressed concern about work/life "balance", asking me if I had enough time to do everything I wanted to do. My answer was always: "Thank God, no. What a dismal thought—to want less than the time you have. You truly savor only that for which you have sacrificed something." That is still how I feel. It is a curse to have time on your hands, it means you do not want enough. The idea of "balance" is an excuse for surrendering to fear and/or laziness.

The problem was with me, on the inside.

And, I lived for others. I was struck when I read the following description: "[A] rule that I had no less devastatingly laid down for myself ... was this: that I had no right to be happy unless the people I loved— especially my children—were happy too. I have come to believe that that is not true. I believe instead that we all of us have ... a kind of sacred commission to be happy... ." Frederick Buechner, *Telling Secrets,* p.102.

In fact, I did not know how to be happy. It was easier to worry about helping others get what they wanted than to figure out what I wanted. Like Buechner, "I had virtually given up doing anything in the way of feeding myself humanly. To be at peace is to have peace inside yourself more or less in spite of what is going on outside yourself." Id., p.25. It was only when I was primarily living by myself, when my wife and daughter moved to France, that I began to make progress.

It has become commonplace to advise one to "care for yourself". I think that that is important, but I also think that it is misunderstood and misused. Love thyself does not to me mean to pamper, spoil or indulge oneself, but to live a life that one can respect and cherish.

So, how then does one love oneself? How does one achieve that inner peace in the midst of chaos?

If I really knew, I would be writing a different book.

But, I do have a few thoughts. Try not to be too hard on yourself. We are all human; temptation can be powerful; and shit happens. Take some time each day to re-establish your bearings, while meditating or exercising or staring into space. Most importantly, evaluate and readjust your positions in relation to others. Fear? Deference? Compulsion to please? Or, to impress? Understand why the opinions of certain people matter to you and ask whether they should. You can be yourself, and be good to yourself, only to the extent you know who you are.

Of course, I have now lost my refuge, my escape hatch. I am not going anywhere. So, I think more, while staying overextended and trying to do more than my body can.

And, the days are still too short.

Peachy-Keen

"All his life,
a little heave of pent-up humour
would now and then shake his burden
into a more comfortable position
upon his bending shoulders."

George McDonald
Thomas Wingfold, Curate
Vol. I, Ch. XVI
(1880)

I have a little joke that has evolved between me and two of my care-givers. When things get difficult, we will say to each other, sometimes with tears in our eyes: "suck it up!" To any casual observer, it would sound bizarre or harsh. But, it is my way of thumbing my nose and laughing at the absurdity of the situation. I think they understand and feel the same.

When a difficult episode is over, they ask "How are you?' I will reply "peachy".

These are efforts to find humor in the challenging circumstances caused by fate. Humor is the best form of active defiance (although, sometimes I do slip into profanity, briefly). We need to laugh at the ridiculousness, and to assert the gloriousness, of life. Even when it is a struggle. I try not to let the atmosphere become too solemn or, God forbid, morbid. But, there is a real pressure on everyone created by the uncertain time line. It is difficult to ignore all the time, but we do get frequent respites. With a good laugh.

I have always used humor to dissipate tensions; although, often it was more ill humor than good humor and generally eased only my tension. It could be quite biting, sometimes unnecessarily cruel. I try to curb that now. These days, in my current situation, I use humor to relax the people around me.

For real friends only.

"Stayin' alive"

"And we're stayin' alive, stayin' alive
Ah, ha, ha, ha, stayin' alive, stayin' alive
Ah, ha, ha, ha, stayin' alive"

The Bee Gees
1977

Unfortunately, I now know a bit about hospitals, from the perspective of the hospital bed, having been two or more times in each of three different ones during a four year period. Actually, many more than two if you count the ERs. One thing is obvious. Hospitals are no place for sick people.

THE PROBLEM

Part of the problem is from trying to do too many different things in one facility. The requirements differ. One size does not fit all. Clearly, there are important advantages and efficiencies in having all capabilities under one roof, so to speak; and I am not advocating physical distancing, only organizational separation. There are at least four distinct functions to be performed: triage and emergency treatment; scheduled surgical procedures; testing; and monitoring and recuperation. It is of this last category that I am most critical.

To the one hospitalized, the operation of the hospital appears rather bizarre. You cannot fathom why things happen as they do. One is awakened every two hours, almost every hour in a shared room. Special needs are ignored. Nothing happens when promised. I have concluded that the explanation is that the operations are organized like most large bureaucracies. Each person, including the doctors, has a specific, rather narrow assigned set of duties and is very resistant to, and institutionally discouraged from, stepping outside of the specified role. The whole operation is itself organized to perform standardized functions, themselves narrowly defined. The rules protect the staff and the institution, as they were designed to do. So little attention is actually paid to the comfort and well being of the patient. The output of the organization seems to be viewed mechanically, to avoid liability while making a profit. There is no feeling that the organization is in the pursuit of a mission or broader goal. It seems to work well for everyone with one exception—the patients.

I was struck while watching a Columbian telenovela, called *La Niña*, much of which took place in a medical school/teaching hospital in Bogota. Many scenes focused on "ethical medicine" and the care of the whole patient, physical and emotional. Care givving. What it should be about. This is clearly the training needed in the United States for nurses.

A SOLUTION?

But, there is one central function that is not being performed today in U.S. hospitals. It is a role once performed by the family doctor. I have called it "health care strategist". We could also say "health care manager". Or, medical advocate, but that may unnecessarily suggest conflict. It ought not to be viewed as adversarial and should seldom be confrontational.

The job is to look at the whole patient—physical state, emotional condition and living circumstances. Then, to try to understand the patient's needs and wishes and next to translate them into a treatment plan. And, finally, to see that plan properly implemented or modified. The need is to interface between the patient and the specialists and among the specialists, to ask questions, to push back, to second guess, to speak up. What a confident, informed and healthy patient would do, if not too scared, intimidated, overwhelmed and ill.

Both the need for and value of such an intermediary are obvious. The problem is how to pay for it or, more precisely, who is to pay for it. It could be a profit generating opportunity for hospitals, improving outcomes, reducing mistakes and attracting patients by improving reputations. But, the whole current situation with insurance discourages such innovation and change. Of course, a similar strategy could work for a health insurer.

MY EXPERIENCE

I am a statistically unusual survivor among ALS sufferers diagnosed in their 60s. The reason I am still writing is because I have had a resource available to the very few—a medical/health advocate. Someone who could communicate my individual needs and circumstances, question the diagnoses and recommendations of the doctors, research my symptoms and proposed treatments and argue for my interests. Someone who cares enough but can still be objective.

She identified a serious allergy (to Bactrim), secured a less dangerous treatment for an inflamed gallbladder (a drain rather removal), which she diagnosed subject to—and confirmed by—a scan, identified a superior treatment to avoid UTIs. In each case, she had to persuade the doctors involved. She also designed my in home care plan.

This "advocate" is my daughter.

For the first two years, I tried to handle things myself. I attended the regional ALS clinic. It was very informative and helpful. The doctors prescribed the durable medical equipment I needed, and it was mostly covered by insurance. They also prescribed physical therapy, which was less successful. In every case, equipment or service, i had to meet with a supervisor who went through a pretty standard questionnaire and interview to confirm or verify what I needed. It was time consuming and tiring.

One such supervisor recommended hospice, where I would get in-home visits, weekly from a nurse and monthly from a doctor, as well as emergency assistance. I signed up. No one had told me that the medical services were limited to keeping me comfortable and did not include life extending procedures or prescriptions. Neither did anyone tell me that I would get a friendly phone call every Friday to see if I was still alive or that hospice was an alternative to hospital treatment under Medicare. I actually had rather enjoyed the regular visits by the nurse, social worker and doctor, all attractive, personable women. And, we acquired a stock-pile of morphine and anti-anxiety drugs. Oh, the ALS clinic canceled my appointments once I enrolled in hospice.

NOW

After about two years, I withdrew from hospice. My daughter took over. Four years ago. She took over checking my vitals. She learned how to change my catheter, then my G-tube (the wonders of YouTube). She figured out how to repair my wheelchair, how to adjust the settings on my BiPap and on my Cough Assist. She arranged to obtain medical supplies online from medical wholesale suppliers. She learned about wound care and prevention. She designed my care routine. And, she trained my caregivers.

"Stayin' alive."

"Another Day"

"Rise and take your stance again
It's he who fights and run away
Live to fight another day"

Bob Marley & The Wailers
The Heathen
(1978)

Everything has gotten more difficult. Especially, clearing my throat and lungs first thing in the morning. And, traversing the sidewalks and streets of Old Town. My ability to communicate has seriously deteriorated. I am even having trouble using my phone to type. When I attempt to talk, I choke and feel a bit nauseous. I tire so quickly. It would be easier to be just a head. Maybe, in a jar. Like Yun Tianming, in *The Three-Body Problem Series* (2014-18) by Cixin Lui.

Oscar has a sixth sense and normally correctly guesses, but new things are a problem. Yami can read my expressions, and she now asks yes/no questions. These two stars caregivers and I have developed some techniques that even Sarah does not know. But, everyone is tired. With a more complicated routine, more mistakes happen. My problem with that is that the two feel badly when mistakes happen, and I am unable to do anything about it. The telephone is a also a problem. The message box has been full for several years. The caregivers do not like to answer the phone, and they don't unless I ask. Thus, we miss most messages.

Toward the end of last year, we discussed my moving to a new condominium to make things easier. No worries about maintenance. More compact space. Less household chores. We could also accelerate the disposal of my possessions and get the house on the market. My son strongly objected, pointing out that they had just moved to a house across the street. He said that he would take over the maintenance. That has not worked. He will do what I specifically ask him to do, but I need more than that. I need someone who notices and takes initiative.

I have tried to handle the house maintenance with Yami and Oscar since December 2021. It has not gone so well. Of course, the house is about 240 years old. I can manage the scheduling, with Yami. But, I cannot supervise or even examine the work done or that needs to be done. Yami does almost all of my errands now (opening mail, paying bills, searching for things, pulling weeds). I ask her to make appointments, ask questions and give instructions. But, I strain to make requests to her or to respond to inquiries through her. I have been able to handle the payroll so far.

Unfortunately, I can be a bit of a freak about orderliness. In my old life, I organized files; I made charts and graphs, I prepared lists. I was never been able to ignore a crooked painting (and have straightened hanging pictures in offices, hotel rooms and hallways in a dozen countries) or tilted lampshade. I got anxious about chipped paint, scratched furniture and cracked glass. I could not resist mending, repairing, adjusting and fiddling.

And, I marveled that others simply do not "see" the blemishes (or, choose to ignore them).

I guess I make it hard to be me.

I do not actually fret about the big things that will require professional help. Such things are expected with an old house. It is the things that I could fix if I could use my arms. Like something dropped on the floor; items we will need left on a counter, where they will inadvertently thrown out; chipped paint, crooked lampshades, unopened mail; unwatered plants; and weeds in the garden. On and on and on.

So, now, how can I possibly cope?

Perhaps, it is good therapy for me to confront and accept imperfection. To stop trying to fix everything. To learn that the flaws do not kill you. Okay, I know that they do not kill me; but, I know, also, that they do not disappear just with time. So. I keep my eyes closed.

I wrote before about learning just to let things happen. It is hard for someone like me, one of the "doers". I am not learning easily.

There is another dimension to the issue now. As I have been losing the ability to speak, I regularly face the choice of whether to try. It is so tempting, should be so easy. A word to warn someone, a word to request something, a word to answer a question. But, most often now, the word is not understood. I am asked to keep repeating to do so, and I try. But, I tire quickly. "Stupid, stupid," I say to myself.

Why, why, why can't you learn? Keep quiet, save your strength.

"Live to fight another day!"

To fight? Yeah, right.
More like, live to run away again.

"Crying"

"Alone and crying, crying
Crying, crying"

Roy Orbison
1962

I cried a little today.

It was the deadline for filing my 2021 tax returns. My tears were not from looking at the sums that I was contributing to the operations of the governments of three states and the Feds. I am reconciled to that. It was from the efforts to sign five filings. (It seems no one can figure out how to create an adequate power-of-attorney for taxes. They apparently prefer a scrawled X.) I need someone to put the pen in my hand, position the paper and place my hand by the line. Then, I strain, I struggle, I collapse, exhausted and nauseous. Three down, two to go.

I feel quite badly for Yami, who assists me. She obviously is aware of my discomfort and frustration. She tries to make it easier, refusing to accept that there is nothing more that she can do—nothing. It creates tensions between us. But, I insisted on also doing my absentee ballot today as well.

I think that the physical consequences are due to the fact that I still have some scattered muscles trying to do what I want against continually increasing resistance. I suspect, but do not know that this experience is different from that of persons who are paralyzed. I am stricken with a feeling of utter, debilitating exhaustion. But, it only lasts a few minutes.

And, I know that I am not alone. But, no one can really help.

My closest prior experience was when I suffered hypothermia. On one my canoe trips with my daughter, we found ourselves paddling for an hour then setting up camp in a steady, cold rain. I foolishly decided not to get a jacket from my pack, not wanting to take the time or to get things wet, I continued in just a cotton sleeveless vest (green). When finally in tent, I could not warm up. Blue and shivering, i could do nothing. My body had quit, shut down. So helpless. I gradually recovered, none the worse for wear. My daughter was not happy with me.

So, now what?

I am not ready to stop doing things. I want more. The particular "more" varies. Sometimes, I really would like to talk, but not all that often. I do not miss eating very much, or even walking. But, I want to continue to take responsibility for my life and circumstances. To be an individual. What does that require physically?

I have been feeling a bit of nostalgia, listening to Don Williams again.

I first heard him with the Poco Seco Singers on an album I purchased my freshman year of college. That and albums by The Chad Mitchell Trio and Glenn Yarborough and the Lamplighters were my favorites. My new friends listened politely and expressed some interest, but my taste was rather unorthodox. In 1966, The Doors and The Rolling Stones were mainstream.

Don is the only one to have a long, successful performing future. And, I love his music. During the 80s, I listened to a lot of country music. I lost touch when New York's country station switched genres. So, I moved on to classical music, especially opera.

It makes me ponder the road I took.

When I was in eighth grade, I was bike riding with two classmates who had made an overture to me. They were not part of the popular group. The one boy said to me that his life ambition was to host a classical music radio program, and he really wished that he had my voice. My voice. At that age, none of us had career goals, and this was the first time I remember someone expressing envy of me.

I had great difficulty in perceiving what someone else thought of me or, more precisely, what their impression of me was. Perhaps, the ambiguity was with me—an enigma.

Freshman year of college, a group of us were lounging in my room drinking beer and listening to my old-fashioned music, when one friend jumped on me and we started to wrestle. He was wiry and strong. My stomach was too full. The result was a draw. Later, as everyone was leaving, one friend said "We were surprised. We expected you to pick him up and toss him across the room." They were disappointed with me. I had not lived up to my image.

I am not sure why these two events stick with me. Memory is very odd. But, both events left me feeling uneasy, knocked a bit off balance.

Curiously, I do not feel "regret" as such. And, certainly not about the type of things one would normally expect to cause regrets. I did stupid things, of course. And, enjoyed some of them. It is perverse, but what I remember too often are my efforts to do the right thing that backfired or that I botched. The memories sometimes keep me awake at night. More than any worries about the future.

The predominant emotion I experience when thinking over my life is disappointment. Weird. But, I feel like I never lived up to my potential. Never quite did it right. Except for my father's eulogy in 2000. That was superb, perfect. Actually, there were a number of less significant speeches, oral arguments and cross-examinations that were also excellent. I think that is why I am disappointed in so much else. I had potential.

Or, maybe not.

Or, maybe, I was just often in the wrong place.

I was not good at office politics, self-promotion, manipulation or even just reading others. Yet, I was in a world where those things mattered, even mattered most. So, I may have been doomed from the start, choosing the wrong goals for my life. Not that I really made a choice, either. I sort of followed the herd. Not literally. I did what was considered the most desired and prestigious. That seemed safe. Do not set your own goals, go with what is recognized by your peers. So, law school, the most recognized New York City law firm, the Upper East Side/Park

Avenue. I knew a lot of people who seemed to know exactly who they were and what they wanted. Generally, they were quite successful.

Actually, in the world in which I lived, most people I encountered were successful, even the neurotics and the deviants.

And, I was successful. Ha!

I have to chuckle.

US

"Are the events I describe
anything like the way they really happened?
As I look back over them,
I think I see patterns, causal relationships,
suggestions of meaning,
that I was mostly unaware of at the time."

...

"I found myself remembering small events
as far back as early childhood
which were even then leading me in something like
that direction but so subtly and almost imperceptibly
that it wasn't until decades had passed
that I saw them for what they were—or thought I did
because you can never be sure whether you are discovering
that kind of truth or inventing it.
The events were often so small that I was surprised to remember
them,
yet they turned out to have been road markers
on a journey I didn't even know I was taking."

Frederick Buechner
Telling Secrets
(1991)

My Ancestry

The name first appears in 1499—a Harpel Bierbrauer in Friedberg in Wetteran (a region partly in Hesse and partly in Prussia), is mentioned as Curator to the Holy Spirit in 1499 and Mayor in 1504. Some 200 years later, there are references to a lawyer and judge named John Jacob Bierbrauer, Councillor and Judge of the Criminal Court in Kassell, born in 1705 in Westerwald, He died on December 4, 1776, in Kassell. A contemporaneous report stated:

"John Jacob Bierbrauer possessed all qualities of a real criminal judge. His remarkable achievements are and will be unforgettable forever, as he not only rid the Hessian country side, but also other lands of swarms of robbers and bandits. He not only discovered their hide-outs but became intimate with them, arrested them, and drove them out of the land, and so secured Hessian safety. Even without methods of torture (which he at least in the case of the Jews did not care to adopt), he, through such methods, had finally gathered a large private criminal archive which was of the greatest aid to him against the 'Scum of the Earth'."

The name also appears in records of students at the University in Marburg in 1565 and 1592. There is a reference to a family Bierbrauer in Bennstein in 1716. A title of nobility was conferred on Dr. Joseph Frederick Bierbrauer in 1782 at Brennstein. Later references to the family can be found in Frankurt a. Main and in Bavaria.

Our interest here is with the descendants of a Philip Bierbruer who lived in Chester County, PA, in the second half of the 18th century, married Elizabeth Stough and had eight children between 1784 and 1799. I can be traced directly back to him, as described below.

The problem is in determining the parentage of that Philip.

OFFICIAL RECORDS

The earliest records in this country show that a Heinrich Bierbauer arrived in Philadelphia on September 26, 1752, aboard the "Richard and Mary", which had sailed from Rotterdam and Portsmouth. He swore allegiance to the Crown. Other records show a Harman (Herman) Beerbower, reportedly born in Germany on July 16, 1741, died in Chester County, PA, on December 29, 1801. A Harman Beerbrower also appears in the First Census of the United States.

A Philipp Kaspar Bierbower was born in Frankurt a. Main on October 29, 1749. He may have come to this country as a boy. It is possible that his father was Johann Jacob Bierbrauer, born July 17, 1713, and married to Margarethe Strauss in 1739.

Tax records show payments in Chester County, PA, between 1756 and 1799, by a Henry Beerbower (also Bearbower, Berbower, Birbower and Bearbouer); between 1762 and 1771, by a Casper Beerbower (also Bearbourer, Bearbower and Bearbrower); between 1774 and 1799, by a Herman Beerbower (also Beerbrower; Bierbrower, Beerbrough, Beerbough, Beebour and Bearbrower) and, between 1774 and 1799, by a Phineas Beerbower (also Bearbrower, Beerbrower and Bearbower).

Tax payments in York County, PA, were made by Philip Beerbower (also Beerbrower and Bierbauer) between 1780 and 1782; by Casper Beerbower (also Bierbrauer and Beerbrower) between 1780 and 1783 and by Jacob Bierbauer in 1782. A Casper Bierbauer took the new oath of allegiance in York County, PA, on May 15,1778.

A Philip Bierbrauer was confirmed in 1776. His father was identified as George Bierbrauer (Casper?).

Casper was a Private in Captain John McMaster's Company, the 7th Class of York County Militia, from 1781 to 1782, providing security at a camp near York holding English prisoners of war. The camp was visited by General George Washington. Phineas Beerbower was a Private in Captain Beatty's Company, Second Battalion, Chester County Militia, commanded by Colonel Thomas Bull in 1780. Harman Beerbower was a Private in Captain Andrew Snyder's Company, Chester County Militia, in 1781.

The early family members were listed generally as either German Reformed Church or Lutheran.

FAMILY LORE

One family report states that a couple with three children, two boys and one girl, came to this country in the 1740s, the girl died in route and the boys were named Casper and Henry. A different report states that a Casper and his brother Philip emigrated to this country in 1752.

Casper Bierbrauer (1736-1822) married Elizabeth Ashenfelter in Carlisle, York County, PA. One family tradition states that Casper came to the New World at age 16 (therefore, in 1752). Another report from Chester County, PA, states that Casper was the brother of Heinrich and that he had four (not three) sons (Henry, Jacob, Casper, Jr., and John). Descendants of a John, reported to be the youngest son of Casper, can be traced from a marriage to Louisa Sheeder in the mid-1810s, with two children Oren John (born 1817) and Ruben (born 1819). Louisa died in 1821. (Both Harman and Philip also had sons named John, born in 1779 and 1785, respectively.) It also appears that Casper resided in Chester County, PA, until 1780, then moved to neighboring York County, PA (or the border between the two counties was adjusted).

There was a Philip living in York County, PA, in about 1780.

The other Beerbowers that appear to have been adults in the United States during the 1770s and 1780s were a Phineas and a Jacob and, perhaps, a George (reported father of a Philip). Phineas lived in Chester County, PA, from at least 1774 to 1799 and was married to Elizabeth. Jacob lived in York County, PA, in 1782. Casper had a son named Jacob, born in 1788, as did Philip in 1784.

(It also appears that a Jacob Philip Bierbrauer, born in 1790, and his wife, Elizabeth Bernes, came from Bavaria in the early 1800s, having nine children between 1816 and 1832, and that another Philip Bierbauer came to the United States in 1840 and married Hannah Fowler in 1843.)

SO?

Attempting to reconcile family oral histories with the documentary records, it may be reasonable to conclude that Herman and Harman and Henry (in the tax records) are one person, who lived in Chester County from at least 1756 until at least 1799. It is conceivable that that person is also the Heinrich who arrived in Philadelphia in 1752. (However, Harman would appear to have been only 11 years old at the time.)

More likely, Heinrich arrived with his wife and two sons, Harman and Casper (ages 11 and 16) in 1752. It is possible that Harman's brother, Casper, was Philip Kaspar born in 1749 in Frankurt a. Main (in which case, Harman would have been the older brother and Casper only four in 1752); although, it is otherwise reported that Casper was born in Germany in 1736.

Unfortunately, we do not have the birth date of the Philip Bierbruer in which we are interested. it would appear that he would have been several years younger than Casper or Harman. If his confirmation in 1776 occurred at the age of 12 or 13 (so his first child would have been born when he was 20 or 21), Philip himself would have been born in 1763 or 1764, more than ten years after Casper and Harman arrived in Pennsylvania. In that case, one could speculate that Philip was the son of Casper from a first marriage and that the record of George, as the father of Philip, could be a mis-recording of Casper. (Elizabeth Ashenfelter was born after 1760, so Casper must not have married her until the late 1770s, when he would have been in his 40s, so a prior marriage is possible.) The absence of any military record for Philip prior to 1788 would seem consistent with a birth in the mid-1760s.

Alternatively, Philip could be the Philip Kaspar born in 1749, in which case he would have been the younger brother of Harman (born 1741) and Casper (born 1736), with all arriving together in 1752. In that case, Philip would have been 27 when confirmed and 36 when his first child was born. (Casper would have been in his mid-40s when his first child with Elizabeth Ashenfelter was born, Harman was probably in his mid-to late-30s when his first child was born.)

Harman Bierbaur and his wife Christiana Hoffman (1747-1826) had a son John Beerbower, born March 10, 1779. John married Elizabeth Fertig in Chester County, PA. Her father, John Fertig, had been born in 1735 or 1736 in Rhineland,Germany. John was a carpenter and farmer and served several years as justice of the peace. He was commissioned by Gov. Simon Snyder as a Captain in the militia, the First Brigade of the Third Division of the Counties of Chester and Delaware, on August 1, 1814. His company, based at Camp Marcus Hook, fought in the War of 1812. John was the father of Sarah Beerbower, who married George Christman, also of German descendent. John died on October 20, 1858, and is buried in the cemetery of the First Reformed Church of Coventry in Chester County.

Casper Bierbrauer had at least five children (Henry, Jacob, Casper, Jr., Elizabeth and Sarah.) Casper, Jr. (1782-1851), married Christina Reiber (1784-1849). A family report states that Henry Bierbrower (the son of Casper), who died in 1823, and his wife, Ann Reed, came from Virginia to Carlisle, PA, and had seven sons and one daughter. They were carriage or wagon makers. Supposedly, a careless painter made a business sign with the second syllable spelled "bow", hence Bierbower. The children were born between 1801 and 1816. The first son, John, was robbed and murdered in New York City in 1838 (reported in the *New York Times*, in one line).

THEREAFTER

In any event, Philip Bierbruer married Elizabeth Stough (Stauch), the daughter of Gottfried and Charlotte Stauch (who had been married in 1754 in a Lutheran church in York County, PA). Philip and Elizabeth had eight children born between 1784 and 1799, including a John, a Sarah, a Philip II and a Peter. Philip served as a Private in the Third Battalion, York County Militia, in 1788. The family moved to Sandy Creek Glades, near Fort Morris in Virginia (now West Virginia) in June 1807. The homestead, with a significant log cabin, was transferred to John in 1811, then to Philip II in 1816, with Peter as a witness to the deed.

Peter Beerbower, born August 23, 1793, married Mary Markley in about 1820. They had six children born between 1824 and 1834. Mary died in 1836 or 1837, and Peter married again shortly thereafter. His second wife was Sophia Sattison. They had nine children, born between 1838 and 1857.The eldest was Peter M.Beerbower II, born August 25,1838.

Peter M. Beerbower II married Amandia Clum in 1860. He served as a Private in Company K, the 150th PA Infantry Volunteers, in the Civil War and was mustered out on June 16,1865.[*] He appears to have lived in Meadville, PA, and then moved to northeast Indiana at the Ohio border. He and Amandia had nine children, born between 1863 and 1885, one of whom was John E. Beerbower, born July 3, 1865. Peter died on December 5, 1907.

John E. Beerbower married Mary Roberta Donat in 1889 and moved across the border to a farm in Carryall Township, Paulding County Ohio, where he lived until his death on March 17, 1934. He was a general livestock farmer. The Donat family was of Dutch and English descent, and both the Donat and Beerbower families attended the Radical United Bretheren Church. John and Mary had three children, Elma, Ira W. and Ralph Isaac, born between 1889 and 1899.

Ralph I. Beerbower was born on November 19, 1899. He married Bernice Swann in 1921. They had three children: Robert Edwin, Martha Jean and Joanne, born between 1922 and 1928. Ralph served in the U.S. Navy in WW I and in the Navy SeaBees in the South PacIfic In WW II.

Robert E. Beerbower was born October 25, 1922, in Hicksville, Ohio. He married Margery Benton in 1947. Robert and Margery had four children, John Edwin, James Norton, JoEllen and Joyce, born between 1948 and 1954. Robert served in the U.S. Army in WW II, commandIng an all Black mortar platoon in Italy. Robert died on June 22, 2000; Margery in August 2013.

This John E. Beerbower, born January 7, 1948, in Columbus, Ohio, married Cynthia Rittenhouse Gibson on August 28,1971. They had two children, John Eliot and Sarah Rittenhouse, born December 13, 1983, and October 9, 1989. (Sarah's DNA shows the strongest genetic connection to Bern, Switzerland, and Hesse, Germany, then England and Ireland.)

John Eliot Beerbower married Megan Lea on August 5, 2012. They have two children, Hannah Elizabeth born March 8, 2016, and Jeffrey Eliot, born December 18, 2018.

---

* Other Beerbowers serving in the Civil War included Jesse, a surgeon in Company H, 3d Regiment Potomac Home Brigade, Maryland Infantry; Samuel Taylor, a private in Company B, 64th Regiment, Ohio Volunteer Infantry; William, the 11th Indiana Zourvas; James C. Bierbouer, a First Lieutenant, Company H,10th Kentucky Calvary Volunteers; Frederick H. Bierbower, a Captain of Company A, 40th Kentucky Infantry; Henry Bierbower, the quartermaster sergeant of Company K, 11th Indiana Infantry; Jonathan Bierbower, a private in Company B, 39th Illinois Infantry; Benjamin, a private in Company I, 3d Pennsylvania Heavy Artillery, under General Butler's command; Andrew Casper, a sergeant in Company H, 23 Iowa Infantry Volunteers (killed June 7, 1863, in action at Milliken's Bend, LA); Sylvester, a private in Company B, 49th Pennsylvania Infantry; and William, a private in Company N, 192d Pennsylvania Infantry.

My First Family

I had what I consider to be a good relationship with my father. He was, like his father, very masculine in appearance and manner (their bald heads and strong jaws, two traits I did not inherit, helped), quiet and soft spoken, of few words, gentle but stubborn. A pillar of strength. I knew he loved me. Yet, he worked hard and when home he often napped with a football game playing on the television. We did not talk much, but I always felt that he was there for the family and for me. Family came first.

Two stories about my father that I told at his funeral. The first. When I was 12, my procrastination caused me to "pull" my first of what would be many "all-nighters" over the next three decades. I had not finished my school project due the next day. I sat alone at the kitchen table, working, while the rest of the family slept. About 1:00 am, my father appeared. He sat with me until I had finished, some two hours later. The second story. Some six years later, on my way home from a date, I was in an accident. The front end of our new Thunderbird was badly damaged. I knocked at my parents' bedroom door a little after 1:00 am (again). When I told my father that there had been an accident, he asked if anyone was injured. I said no. He rolled over and went back to sleep.

My relationship with my mother was more complicated. She was pretty in the fashion of the 1950s and very competent. A true partner with my father. As I was her first child, she doted on me. She took great interest in my reading and then my school work. We talked endlessly. She encouraged my interests in art and in crafts. She also nudged me into activities by conspiring with my teachers and signing me up if I did not violently object. I turned to her when I needed help or advice.

For example, when I was starting 10th grade at Oakwood High School, in the town to which we had just moved, a very attractive girl approached me at my locker, introduced herself, and then invited me to go swimming with her that afternoon. I was sure she was older than I was. But, I was in AP math, so the algebra book I was carrying would normally be carried by a junior. I mumbled an excuse and said I would see her after lunch. This was exactly the type of situation I desperately feared: I would awkwardly tell her I was just 15, she would be embarrassed, I would be humiliated. And, I would suffer every time I saw her again. I went home for lunch and threw myself on my mother for help. She calmly made a few phone calls. The young lady was a senior! However, she was young for her class and had previously been dating a junior. But, I was a sophomore. But, someone now would tell her privately about my age. I was saved! In the event, the young lady was incredible. She came up and said, "I suspect you don't drive, so how about I pick you up?" We went swimming. She was at least as good a swimmer as I was. I still regret that I had not been confident enough to have pursued her. (I did not then realize that my cautiousness—cowardliness—would just get worse, resulting in repeated such missed opportunities.)

However, there was something not quite right, something that made me uneasy about my mother. Perhaps, a character flaw of some sort, a bit of a social climbing instinct. Years, no, decades, later, I recognized that she was inclined to be a serious gossip and unkindly judgmental. But, that changed as she reached old age, fortunately. And, we got along well again at the end.

When I was 6 or 7, with a brother and almost two sisters, my parents undertook to build a house in Northville, Michigan, acting as the contractor and doing a lot of the unskilled work. Our weekends were spent on a wooded lot turning into a construction site. Mother would pack a picnic lunch and then struggle to keep three small children and a baby safe. We moved, along with the brother of my father's brother-in-law, a carpenter who was to build our kitchen cabinets, into an unfinished house, living in the large bottom floor room divided up into "rooms" by metal storage cupboards and shelving. One working bathroom. No kitchen. We ate most of our meals at the Old Mill restaurant in the center of this village of some 10,000 people.

The house turned out very well, and we enjoyed many years there.

My parents appeared to be good friends and real partners. When we kids were old enough to be alone, they spent a half hour together talking before we all sat down to eat. I think they discussed each of their days, my father's problems as well as my mother's.

I remember a family trip when I was about 8 or so. It was to somewhere in the northern part of Michigan's Lower Peninsula, but I do know where or who we were visiting. I know we drove (the only type of trip in those days), and we had a Ford convertible with the round taillights and of an odd pinkish-beige color. We were with a young engaged couple at a racetrack. The young man raced stock cars. He took my brother and me for a couple laps around the track. It was my first and only ride in a car with no passenger seats and which one entered through the glassless side window. Later, as the rest of us sat on a hill overlooking the track, my parents drove around the track in the Ford with the top down. Watching them, the young woman said to her fiancé, "Do you think we will be as happy as Marge and Bob?"

Our family was very close physically. We took family vacations, ate dinner together, went to church together, went to the swimming club together, visited our grandparents and cousins together. Many, many trips with six in the car.

My brother and I did many activities together. However, perhaps because of the age differences, we were never emotionally close. We did not ever talk and certainly never confided in one another. By the time my sisters began school, I was consumed by my own narrow world. They were irrelevant outside of my family. I did not really know any of my siblings until we were all on the wrong side of middle age.

Our neighbors had boys of ages between my brother and me and one a year older. I was split between a group that was a bit too young and a boy a bit too old. I did some very interesting things with the older boy —building things, conducting experiments, exploring the abandoned orchard and gravel pit nearby. But, he also liked to bully me sometimes, so it was up and down. In junior high, our family became very good friends with a family that had two boys, one my class and one a year ahead, and a girl the age of my sister. I became quite close with the two boys. My brother found his own friends.

Because my wife disliked my family and was engaged in open hostilities with my mother, I saw my family members only infrequently for ten years. That changed somewhat when my children were born and even more so when my father got sick. We all visited frequently during his last three years. I was able to say goodbye by telephone during his last hour. Then, the kids and i visited my mother regularly during what turned out to be her last four years; and, when, in 2013, she began to fail, I was able to make four trips from the U. K. to visit. I was able to say goodby shortly before the end.

Since my wife died and I moved to Virginia, I have seen a lot more of my siblings and gotten to know them as people. A lot of surprises, and many of them pleasant.

My Second ..., But, Then Again

"A narcissistic mythomaniac?"
...
"[A]n uncanny ability to read
other people's emotional states...
to intuit hopes and insecurities
that others thought well-hidden[,]
made her equally adept
at charming people
and at wounding them."

Robert Galbraith
The Ink Black Heart

"if you are beautiful enough you don't really
have to be anything much else ... .
You don't have to be ... kind or unselfish
or generous or compassionate... ."

Frederick Buechner
Telling Secrets

I feel the need to say something more about my wife.

(I would title this essay "On the Other Hand", but there is no "on the one hand". As a devotee of Fowler's *Dictionary of Modern English Usage*, I cannot use the second hand without the first, just as I carefully avoid split infinitives and make ample use of commas. So, we make do.)

She was certainly beautiful as a young woman (and remained so; although, my perception of her attractiveness changed). But, what most strongly attracted me was her apparently unflappable self confidence and clear sense of direction. She was also a skilled listener, who could charm intense conversation out of even the most reserved and boring man and mesmerize the biggest nerd.

When with her, my own awkward insecurities disappeared. I was confident in restaurants, bold at parties, almost invincible in social settings. It was a new experience for me, and a very heady one. Her interests and ambitions were quite exciting and eye opening. Without a doubt, she ignited my interest in paintings, sculpture, design and architecture. (But, my passion long outlasted hers.) In all events, she motivated and enabled a much more adventurous, ambitious and striving life for me. I began to want.

I do not mean to suggest that I did not feel stirrings of ambition or covetousness before her. When I was 10 or so, my parents took my brother and me to Key Biscayne, Florida. It was my first time on an airplane. My father was attending a conference that started the next day which was also when the hotel room was available. So, we took an evening flight then slept in the rental car. At dawn, we had donuts and juice in a large botanical garden. I was utterly mesmerized by the exotic plants surrounding us. I decided then that I wanted to travel and see new things. About five years later, we took a family road trip, visiting the enormous Biltmore mansion in Asheville, NC, and then the spectacular original Vanderbilt house on Fisher Island, Florida. I was completely hooked on grand architecture and became determined to see the cathedrals, castles and stately homes of the Old World.

It was another ten years before I, with the help of my wife, begin realizing that dream.

She also challenged my values and self-image. She advocated objectives and behavior that were inconsistent with my Midwestern middle class prejudices. She caused me to question and then to doubt many of my beliefs. Of course, this was occurring while I was an undergraduate student already encountering quite challenging influences. She was acutely aware of societal hierarchy and was intent on moving up it. That made me uncomfortable; but, upon reflection, I concluded that, as sins go, social climbing was not so bad.

One development while we were dating was her telling me that her father was violent and abusive at home, to her and to her mother. On a couple of occasions, she called me late at night frightened of him, and asked me to stay on the phone with her until morning, which I did. Once, she called and asked me to rescue her from one of his rages. She lived about 20 miles away. I drove there. One of my friends, who was drawn to drama, followed me in his car, bringing a golf club in case of violence. She came running out and jumped in with me. I am not sure anyone other than me ever knew Mike was there. I never knew the truth. Her father was a problem drinker. Her parents fought a lot and several times separated then got back together. She said several times that her mother was hospitalized with injuries he inflicted. But, I do not know. Certainly, these events were far beyond my experience, and I came to view myself as her savior.

She also had, with me in private, an innocent, playful, almost child-like side. It was something that I hoped would reappear from time to time after we married. It did not. it disappeared completely.

After we married, I discovered that my frugality was a source of serious conflict. Again, I slowly conceded she had a point. Within a couple of years of finishing graduate school, however, her spending was causing me to lose sleep. We were living well beyond our means. But, our incomes kept going up. In addition, it was the late '70s when rampant inflation penalized savings and rewarded debt, undermining the things my parents had taught me.

To some extent, I was lost already. My father was very disappointed that instead of doing something productive, something that built or produced physical things of value, I had become a lawyer—a parasite or, euphemistically, a societal transaction cost. At the time, none of us ever even could imagine what society would be willing to pay for transaction costs some 10 years later. I was then to become what my father had despised, as the practice of law changed from a profession to more of a confidence game. My father, however, had mellowed in the meantime (my parents having themselves tasted some of the "good life").

I was to learn, curiously to me (actually, to my stunned shock), my wife's apparent confidence and purposefulness hid a deep and destructive insecurity, combined with the a compulsion to mislead. Her mother had diligently hidden their family personal and financial problems from the world, something I recognized but did not really understand while we were dating. After we were married, social climbing became an obsession of my wife's. She began regularly to misrepresent our economic status and to spend to prove the falsehoods. Keeping ahead of the "Jones's" became a passionate, consuming pursuit.

We needed bigger and more prestigious apartments every couple of years. We secured what for the time was an unprecedentedly large personal loan (the "better" coops were "all cash", no mortgages). As it happened, we were exceptionally talented at design and the City real estate market was very robust. We made a lot of money.

One of the most distressing things to me was my wife's vulnerability to snooty salespeople. Anyone could make her feel inadequate, prompting her—no, compelling her—to buy. She became such a target that luxury stores would just send her expensive dresses, many of which she kept and paid for regardless of the look. She also suffered more than her share of thefts. Handbags, wallets, credit cards, bank deposits. Obviously, skilled crooks could spot her as an easy victim.

She dealt with me by going into a state of destructive depression that would last for days.

I succumbed. I found myself scrambling to hide the situation from the outside world. The first time, I was in shock. This was not the person I knew; this was not a situation I understood; this was not something I was prepared to handle or even prepared with which to cope. It was very traumatic. I did learn how to stand it (barely), but never how to deal with it. She pretty much got her way.

At the same time, I started to enjoy spoiling myself, indulging in luxury, having the best. In truth, I became hooked, addicted. I was embarrassed with and ashamed of myself, but I attempted to rationalize and excuse my behavior. Between the very dark episodes, there was excitement and adventure and indulgence.

But, she began encountering difficulties and conflicts at work. I tried to help, to talk her through the personality clashes, to help her do her work. I was over my head in both areas. Later, she became attracted to people and businesses on the fringes of financial legitimacy. Her creativity and her addiction to exaggeration opened doors and generated opportunities.

I thought it was sleazy, but I negotiated her contracts and revised her drafts. She made millions (and did not go to jail like some of her business partners), but I had to draft complaints and demands to initiate legal proceedings twice for her to collect. Typical in that world. Surprisingly, the experience just made her more reckless, more attracted to "swindlers" and more vulnerable to exploitation.

My influence slowly evaporated. She did not "need" my advice nor my help. I was a wimp, too conservative and uptight..

Her last big project was a financial failure. Egged on and manipulated by a charming, self-dealing decorator who claimed to be a Count, and over my increasingly strident and futile objections and warnings, she invested heavily in a property renovation with frenzied excess. Much more than could ever be re-cooped. In the end, I took the loss, as the survivor. Actually saved some taxes.

My Next Family

I always just assumed that I would have children. I did not think about it much. Then, approaching 35, it became a subject of discussion and a source of some friction. My wife declared that she would be happier without. I pondered the question for weeks, and I concluded that I really did want a family with children. I was open to waiting and adopting, if she preferred.

She subsequently announced that she was ready to try. I have since suspected that she was concerned that I might leave. I do not think that it was in my conscious mind at the time, but I have come to believe that it was then a real possibility. She was very perceptive and could read the cards far better than I could at that age.

The first one came easily, at least the conception. Probably, first try. The pregnancy was relatively easy, except that my wife disliked our highly recommended obstetrician. The labor was long, however. Almost 24 hours.

I was in middle of a trial at the time. Fortunately, it was a bench trial. While I was at the hospital, the Chairman of the company on the other side gave his direct testimony. Then, over his protest, the judge adjourned for the day. When I got home that evening, the transcript was waiting. I had a drink or two, then studied the testimony. After a shower and shave, I went to court and cross-examined the Chairman.

(This was not the only birth during a trial for me. In Wilmington, Delaware, on the first day of trial, when I was to give my opening statement, I got up early and went for a run to relax. Coming back up the hill to the Dupont Hotel, I saw my two associates rush out, jump into a taxi and disappear. Fortunately, I was pretty relaxed from my run. A couple of hours later, as I stood to begin my rather long opening, I was handed a message and was able to announce to the court and large audience that Elise had safely delivered her baby. My other associate, Marc, who had taken her to the hospital, appeared shortly thereafter in the courtroom.)

My second child was the opposite. We spent months trying to conceive. After a relatively early miscarriage, apparently of twins, we went to a specialist we determined we were both functioning properly and suspect one of us harbored an asymptomatic virus adversely affecting implantation. Following a course of powerful antibiotics for both of us, my wife promptly conceived, and our daughter was born after a very short labor.

We had baby nurses and nannies, all of whom were very helpful, but it was a big change having other people so much in our family life. We traveled frequently with our son. The Grand Canyon, England, France, Italy. He was an easy travel companion, except for some carsickness. He would eat anything and slept soundly in his portable cot. In New York City, he became my constant weekend buddy. We walked all over Central Park exploring. We frequently visited the Metropolitan Museum of Art, went to The City Ballet Sunday afternoons (where he had a favorite candy) and went on day trips out of the City.

He was a very good looking toddler. Beautiful, thick blond hair, a full round face, wonderful coloring. His mother, however, dressed him like an Edwardian poster boy. He could have had a role in *Bridgerton* if it had been filmed 35 years ago. Gradually, he rebelled against it.

Nursery school was a difficult time for him. He just did not fit in well. That was to be the pattern. I failed to deal with it effectively.

He was very cooperative, but seldom enthusiastic or even happy. I thought that he was so solemn because his English nanny was a bit dour. But, I probably missed a lot. Once, while driving through the Loire Valley in France, with my wife complaining loudly, threatening to go home taking him with her, he said, "Daddy, couldn't we have another child for Mommy to take?" He was almost four.

Our daughter was born just before our son turned six. He was very excited. Then, we suffered an family upset. On his first day of real school, I woke early. I heard the elevator stop at our landing, but no one rang the bell. I had a terrible premonition. I looked out and there was a letter addressed to me. From our nanny, quitting with no notice because she could not stand anymore how my wife treated her. I hid the letter, got everyone up, fixed breakfast. Then, we walked him to school, with my wife ranting about how irresponsible his nanny was for missing the first day of school. I told him that I would pick him up at lunch time. That apparently was the she suspected what had actually happened. Of course, she was outraged.

I spent quite a bit of time with him over the next week. He never asked what had happened to his nanny. I explained that she did not have time to help us anymore. He remained quiet about it. Still is.

I took him to spend a father/son weekend at a boy's camp in Hunt, Texas, as a possibility for the next summer (1993). We had a good time, and he indicated that he would like to go. The whole family took him down and picked him up. There was a bit of a stir; seems he was their first camper from east of Tennessee. I do not know what happened, but he was quite uncommunicative about his month there.

The next school year was in Washington, D. C., which he did not want. Then, a summer camp in Colorado with more urban boys. One of his cabin mates was killed in a horse riding accident, and the camp brought in counselors for the boys (and parents). Again, he said nothing to me.

By the time we returned to New York two years later, I saw that his relationship with his sister had soured. When she was three or four, he was devoted to her and protective of her. A few years later, he seemed resentful and bitter, and he reacted to her provocations violently Somewhere, I had clearly failed. But, the failure snuck up on me. I still cannot figure out what went wrong or even when.

My daughter was a very different personality and was so from the beginning. Seldom serious, always on the move, getting into everything, especially her brother's stuff. Although, she now has a remarkably symmetrical face, as a small child, she was a bit lopsided. Very impish in looks, as well as behavior. She was also much more social and outgoing. We came to calling her "The Mighty Sarah" when she was about 3. She would climb up on a footstool and strike a "Mighty Mouse" pose—feet apart, face tilted up and fist raised. That captured her personality and spirit.

Like with my son, I saw her with other kids only occasionally. I took the two of them to Central Park, to the circus and around the neighborhood. However, we then rented a house in the country. So, weekends were mainly family. We swam, explored and went for drives. My daughter did make some friends in the neighborhood, even though the houses were far apart.

In mid-1993, my wife and children moved temporarily to Georgetown. I visited weekends and occasionally during the week. In 1994, I was involved in a major bankruptcy filed in Delaware and the principal opposing counsel were in D. C. So, it was convenient. I took the kids all around the District. We picnicked in gardens, my son and I biked all over.

Actually, during the first autumn, I was taking depositions in San Jose, California. I would fly back Friday nights on the red eye, landing at Dulles a little after 5:00 am. When I would get to the house, my daughter would greet me. We began what became a tradition. While the others slept, she and I would buy poppyseed/lemon muffins, coffee and juice and go down to the canal and enjoy an early breakfast.

When the kids moved back to New York with me, we made breakfast out once a week a ritual for the three of us, adopting a local coffee shop run by Greeks as our place. For the first year back, my daughter's first year of real school, I took her to school each morning and tried to attend all of the school events. My son could walk the four blocks to his school.

Although we three spent a lot of time together, the kids grew further and further apart, with frequent conflicts for a couple of years (11 and 6, at this point). I also felt more distanced from them. My son was even more withdrawn, and my daughter became absorbed into the social scene at school. She was attracted to the more outgoing girls, who were also the less serious students and the most cliquish. I was concerned that she was becoming too susceptible to peer pressure, but how do you get a 9 year old girl to embrace eccentricity?

But, the next phase was the most difficult for me. She became secretive. Or, more precisely, she kept things secret from me. That was when I realized and mourned the fact that she was growing up. A young girl/woman doing things about which she did not want to tell her father. Of course, I had been blind. It was not until she had a problem, about which she fortunately was brave enough to tell me, that I awoke to my children's worlds. Well, I should say "got a glimpse of".

After my last year of high school and, again, after my freshman year of college, I went with friends canoeing in Quetico Provincial Park just above Minnesota. It was true wilderness camping. You, your packs and the canoe. Almost 25 years later, on an airplane with my son, I saw an article in the Delta magazine about canoeing in the Boundary Waters, just adjacent to Quetico. I showed my son. He showed some interest, so i asked if he would like to go. He said yes. The next summer, the two of us disappeared into the North Woods by canoe. We were to take three such trips, each more challenging. For the next two, we went by float plane to a far corner of the Park to begin our trip. Consequently, in the three trips we saw most areas of the acre wilderness.

He was an able camper, tireless on the portages carrying two Duluth packs, helpful with the camp, a capable fisherman and never complaining. But, I felt like he never really enjoyed it, was never really happy. And, we did not talk much.

A few years later, when she became a teenager, I took my daughter on three such [canoe] trips. She was as tough as her brother, and as weak a paddler. She disliked fishing but got as excited as I did about exploring campsites, seeing bald eagles and loons, encountering waterfalls and anticipating the next lake. We talked endlessly. About the profound experience of being completely on one's own, with no contact with the rest of the world—no news, no clock, no phone, no help. Fully responsible for one's own life, and each other's. We talked about life, the world, our philosophies. The last trip was for two weeks. We had trouble returning.

In 2011, I began my retirement with a week at Red Mountain Resort in southern Utah. I took my daughter. It was supposed to be three of us, but my wife backed out at the last minute, as had become our normal. As a result, we enjoyed a large two bedroom suite. To my puzzlement, on our first morning hike, after we had introduced ourselves by name only, no would talk to us. The second day, I introduced myself as Sarah's father. We were greeted warmly by everyone. The unaccompanied women seemed particularly pleased that she was not my fourth wife. It seemed only the day before when servers refused her a beer. She had grown up, and apparently was gorgeous. Poor Dad.

All in all, the City was a tough place to be a parent or to be a child.

OTHERS

"To love our neighbors
as we love ourselves
means also to love ourselves ... .
It means to treat ourselves
with as much kindness and understanding
as we would the person next door ... .
Little by little then
we begin to be able
to look at each other's faces,
and at our own faces in the mirror,
without the intervening shadows
that unaired secrets cast."

Frederick Buechner
Telling Secrets
(1991)

Peter

Not the Saint, but Laurence J. (originator of the Peter Principle).

I find we are surrounded by mediocrity and incompetence. Why? Are my current expectations and standards just too unrealistic? Has my memory been warped? Perhaps, the child just did not notice the mistakes, the blundering.

Over the years, I have been the direct supervisor for more than 200 people, at least half of whom were lawyers. I also interviewed several hundred applicants for jobs. The strongest lesson from these experiences was that people vary dramatically in their abilities. There are, of course, the differences in personal physical and behavioral characteristics, which have an effect on performance; but, more importantly, there is something else that makes certain individuals stand out, far above the others. While the bulk of the people fall along a continuum from useless to useful, a handful are qualitatively different, with an unbridgeable gap in between.

The rare few bring initiative, insight, instinct and creativity to every task. They "own" the work. They feel deeply responsible for the results. For their own assigned tasks and for the tasks of others that affect the outcome. They are perfectionists; they care. Intelligence certainly matters, but it seems supplementary to this other something.

The other takeaway is that the critical extra something is very difficult to ascertain during an interview (I was never able to master the skill), but its presence or absence would generally become obvious very quickly on the job. For the quiet or shy, it can take a little longer, but the presence or absence is unmistakable. The fact is that some people are markedly better than others at almost everything. Fortunately, the most able and effective do not all have the same interests or aspirations. The result is that they are scattered among vocations.

I was convinced in 1970 by the relevance of the Peter Principle: that within hierarchies, people get promoted until they reach jobs that they cannot adequately do, to their position of incompetence. I think, however, it is not a universal truth but a phenomenon of the second half of the twentieth century.

Of course, for it, we need employment structures with hierarchical positions that can be filled from below. We need the practice of often filling positions from within. And, ironically, we need a relative meritocracy. If employment is based on family, or connections or political correctness (in the traditional sense); then there will be different outcomes.

So, the crafts and trades will operate differently, as will family businesses and entrepreneurial start-ups and small business. Even large organizations with more entrepreneurial and innovating mindsets will avoid the Peter Principle. The most susceptible will be administrative offices, retail banks, insurance companies, government departments and bureaucracies generally.

People in the nineteenth century took a very different view.

For example,

"[The garden's] preservation was owing merely to the fact that their gardener was blessed with **a wholesome stupidity rendering him**

incapable of unlearning what his father, who had been gardener there before him, **had had marvellous difficulty in teaching him. We do not half appreciate the benefits to the race that spring from honest dulness.** The CLEVER people are the ruin of everything."

George McDonald, *Thomas Wingfold, Curate*, Vol. I, Ch. VII (1880) (emphasis added).

Of course, people earned their livelihoods quite differently in the nineteenth century. Large numbers were self employed, many as farmers, skilled tradesmen and shopkeepers. Few worked in bureaucracies. For many workers, there was a quite direct and unmistakable link between how well they performed and the survival of their families. Mistakes had visible consequences. You knew if you screwed up. And, your family and neighbors knew. It was a more fragile, more vulnerable and more transparent existence .

In addition, many children learned trades or useful skills from their parents. Occupations were passed from one generation to the next. People learned how to do things. They achieved proficiency. All one needed was common sense coupled with a strong sense of responsibility.

Industrialization resulted in more and more working in factories and on assembly lines. Much has been written about the resulting alienation of these workers, but, at least, they knew when they made a mistake and they could see and feel the output of their collective labors. Compare that to today's typical office workers.

In the twenty-first century, for a variety of reasons, including the explosion of employment litigation, many office workers and bureaucrats are largely sheltered from consequences of poor performance. The injuries from their mistakes are borne by others--customers, employers, coworkers. They are also still separated from the output of the enterprise. Not surprisingly, many feel little commitment, loyalty or, even, responsibility toward their work. They do the minimum, focused on their rights and benefits. Pay is an entitlement, not something earned.

Where to now?

"One way or another"

"One way or another,
I'm going to find ya,
I'm gonna get ya,
get ya, get ya, get ya"

Blondie
1979

Now, over thirty years later, reading the lyrics, I see that the song reflects a stalker. Listening to it over the years, I could understand only a few of the words, mainly just the first four. But, the frenzied rhythm was addictive.

Now, in 2022,the song haunts me in a different way. I am no longer the pursuer (or predator) but am the pursued, the victim. Chased by what? The government? Sometimes, it feels that way. The mainstream media? Sort of. A political or cultural movement? That is closer.

I pay my taxes, averaging around 30% of my gross income over 40 years. Probably, close to 40% if one includes property and sales taxes. (The percentage went up with the 2017 "tax cut for the wealthy".) I am also pretty generous, in recent years donating about 10% of my gross to charity and gifting another couple percent (up from 10% of after-tax income). I am leaving about a third of my accumulated assets to charity.

I have been very well off, not private jet/Lamborghini well off, but quite fortunate. The last couple of years, I have had to devote about a third of my gross to medical expenses, including in-home care, reducing my income taxes some. But, I live nicely on the remaining 20-25%. I have lived the American Dream.

So, why do I feel pursued or threatened or, more accurately, harassed? Well, I am an old wealthy white man--today's favorite scapegoat? Maybe. Not that I feel endangered. It is more like the nuisance of mosquitoes than the threat of a lethal predator. (Although, I wonder, can one die of a thousand paper cuts?) Perhaps, it is just the normal feeling of the old facing change.

Yet, I cannot help but wonder what it is like for people with values and perspectives similar to mine but without the safety net I was able to build. Economic hardship can certainly sharpen one's sense of vulnerability.

I see that my values and identity are being attacked. I am in the 1% that does not pay its "fair share"; although, I think I do. I must reexamine myself to recognize that I am a creature of privilege, not of sacrifice, hard work and ability. I should renounce my embedded racism, even though race played no part in my upbringing. Many of my books are censured, my history is revised, my heroes are rejected. My conceptions of duty, responsibility, charity and integrity are all being mocked.

I felt like an outsider in college, of course, since I questioned the prevailing orthodoxy. I kept quiet at my law firm; although, not completely disguised—when an administrative or policy matter needed a bipartisan veneer, the partners turned to me. But, it seems only the last few years that differences of view are condemned rather than celebrated, that the cultural and intellectual heritage of Western civilization is being disparaged, that uniformity and conformity are being promoted, even demanded.

We see the demise of self-reliance and hard work; they are scorned, no longer admirable characteristics. "Quiet quitting" dominates. And, work/life balance? Yes, but, what is the "life"? Television, video games and social media? Is the result just no meaningful work nor meaningful life?

Entitlements are today's game. Government entitlements, employment entitlements, minority entitlements and individual entitlements. Today, we do not have obligations, we are owed; no one is to be responsible for one's own problems; there is always someone, some group or just society at large to blame.

I can not quite come to grips with the events concerning Gibson's Bakery and Oberlin College. The initial student reaction can be dismissed as a result of immaturity and peer group pressure, as much as to prejudices and lack of judgment. But, the facts came out pretty quickly. The three blacks were attempting to steal and resorted to violence to try to escape. Yet, the boycott and false accusations continued--the students even doubled down, and enjoyed the support of the College administration.

The College defended its behavior at the subsequent trial in which the Bakery claimed damages for injury from several types of tortious conduct. The responsible course of action would have been to apologize for the obvious "mistake" and offer to settle. The jury returned a verdict for the Bakery, awarding substantial compensatory damages and huge punitive damages. What did the College do? Declared that it would fight on to vindicate itself. Only after losing its appeal to the Ohio State Supreme Court, its last realistic resort, six years later, did the College announce that it had decided to pay the judgment against it. Apparently, the amount will come from the endowment, and the College President and the Dean of Students will suffer no consequences except for reputational damage from the publicity.

One can only wonder: "Where were the Trustees?" They are supposed to provide the wisdom and moral guidance when the institution goes astray, are they not?

One can hope that it was a case of bias crowding out judgment and not the conscious pursuit of a personal or political agenda.

I wonder the same thing about our current Administration's position on inflation. Presumably, President Biden just follows instructions, but Secretary Yellan or Chairman Powell? I was writing about the dangers of the inflationary pressures almost two years ago in *Wanderings*. And, the results are turning out much worse than I then feared, as the stock market appears to have finally realized the week of September 13, 2022.

Where are our supposed leaders? Or, are some of Trump's propensities contagious?

We learned this September that the Russians have spent some $300 million in the last few years to confuse and distort democratic elections around the world. We also learned that the Democrats here are spending millions of dollars to distort the outcomes of various Republican primaries. So, Putin's values are contagious too?

What is particularly annoying is that I am viewed as irrelevant, apart from my money. Politicians used to compete for the middle, to try to appeal to the moderate. No more. On both sides, the strategy is to appeal to the base, which means moving to the extremes. One might wonder why that makes any sense. The reason is the rather low voter turnout in the U. S. With 40% of potential voters not showing up, the premium is on getting out the vote among those who generally sympathize with your end of the political spectrum, and it is believed that increasing the perceived differences between the parties will energize the base. Get out the vote. Except among the moderates, who become more inclined to stay home out of frustration or disgust.

The 2016 election is often explained in terms of the alienation of white working class men. They certainly had been suffering. But, the alienation extended much more broadly. And, I think it is getting worse. After a successful Trojan Horse campaign for the Presidency, the Democrats behaved like sharks smelling fresh blood. It was very depressing. I could never vote for Trump because he lacks common decency and is proud of it. But, he is now mimicked on both sides of the aisle. The situation is very poor for reasoned decision making.

At one time, a person could essentially opt-out of politics and just live one's life. But, today, the government will not let you. It is so big and so pervasive that it cannot be ignored. There are always forms to be completed and filed, taxes to be paid, regulations to be navigated, laws to be deciphered. So, it is necessary to participate.

But, vote?

How do you get candidates that you want to support?

That is a hard, very hard question.

But, beware.

"I'm gonna get ya,
get ya, get ya, get ya."

Bull shit.

It ain't over yet

Empathy

Two years ago, I wrote:

"I have now come to believe that the greatest virtues are empathy and humility—reflected in the recognition that 'there but for the grace of God, go I.' (Empathy is what I think is meant by Christian love for 'thy neighbor'.)"

It is curious to me that in the Bible, love of self is taken as a given. It is even presented as a benchmark or standard for how one should treat others.

> "Love thy neighbor as thy self."
> *Leviticus* 19:18.; Mark 12:31.

> "Therefore all things whatsoever ye would that men should do to you,
> do ye even so to them... ."
> *Matthew* 7:12.

The goal is to see oneself in others and to treat them accordingly. Empathy.

Do we have more empathy today, in the twenty-first century?

I was struck by the story of Lazarus and the rich man (*Luke* 16:19-31). The rich man lives a life of abundance, never even noticing

Lazarus suffering right outside his door. They both die. The rich man burning in Hades sees Lazarus with Abraham resting in complete comfort. He asks a very modest favor (a drop of water).

> "Father Abraham, have mercy on me, and send Lazarus,
> that he may dip the tip of his finger in water, and cool my tongue;
> for I am tormented in this flame."

But, he is denied.

> "Son, remember that thou in thy lifetime receivedst thy good things,
> and likewise Lazarus evil things:
> but now he is comforted, and thou art tormented."

Oddly, by today's standards, Lazarus does not protest and blame others for causing his situation, he does not ascribe his circumstances to his environment or to society, he does not whine or beg or, even, argue. Instead, he asks if Lazarus could return to Earth and warn his five brothers so they might avoid his fate. He thinks of others, *albeit* siblings. Not a very American twenty-first century reaction to suffering. ("Abraham saith unto him, 'They have Moses and the prophets; let them hear them.' ")

Noble Prize winning physicist Frank Wilczek opines that:

> 'Based on experience and consensus, people have gradually abandoned old views and adopted new ones. Thus, it is fair to say that, judged by experience and consensus, the new views are improvements on the old ones. ...A common theme in all these developments **is a widening circle of empathy. With progress, we've come to consider people and creatures as having intrinsic value and being worthy of profound respect, just like ourselves.''**

Fundamentals (2022), p.227 (emphasis added).

Really?

I agree that we now have a more expansive and inclusive view of who is our neighbor, but I would not equate that with increased empathy. By its nature, empathy is an individual, not a societal, phenomenon. People feel empathy, not societies.

Wilczek quotes what he calls "a kind of credo" of Albert Einstein:

> "**A human being is part of a whole,** called the Universe, a part limited in time and space. He experiences himself, his thoughts and feelings, as **something separated from the rest, a kind of optical delusion of his consciousness. This delusion is a kind of prison for us.**"

Id., p.228.

Is Einstein right? If so, is our consciousness the source of our greed, of our inhumanity, by reason of that delusion of. separateness?

Of course, these questions are not within the normal expertise of physicists. So, I looked to contemporary anthropologists for guidance. It was a bit of a surprise.

> "When archaeologists undertake balanced appraisals of hunter-gatherer burials from the Palaeolithic [more than 10,000 years ago], they find high frequencies of health-related disabilities – but also surprisingly high levels of care until the time of death (and beyond, since some of these funerals were remarkably lavish). ... [I]n origin, it might be claimed, our species is a nurturing and care-giving species... ."

David Graeber and David Wengrow, *The Dawn of Everything: A New History of Humanity* (2021), p.14.

Crude stone tool use arose about 2.5 million years ago; *Homo sapiens* appeared between 300,00 and 200,000 years ago; artistic expression, about 40,000 years ago; empathy, more than 10,000 years ago. What about consciousness? There seems to be no way to know.

But, it appears that consciousness enabled empathy, rather than retarded it.

Consciousness made us aware of ourselves, gave us time, enabled us to imagine the future, to capture the past, to sense the eternal and to recognize the presence of life, and even of humanity, in others—the foundations of empathy.

Safety

Curiously, old town Alexandria has seemed to me to be an unusually safe place. Almost like Cambridge, England. I have lived in places in which i was often scared.

I started my adult life in the New York City of the 1970s. One felt uncomfortable in the neighborhood bodegas, on alert on the subway, wary of approaching groups of teenagers. I had just spent 12 months in England during the IRA period, so I was accustom to being alert and avoiding unaccompanied parcels and bags on the street, as well as doing without trash receptacles on the street. So, I did not sit by the door on the subway, avoided using payphones on the street and tried not to pat my wallet in public places. Of course, the City then was much worse for women, who were vulnerable to sexual assault in any crowded and confined place. (Our only City burglary occurred after the streets had become much safer.)

i learned not to park on the street. One night, instead of going to my garage, I parked right in front of my Park Avenue building to save time the next morning--passenger window shattered, radio gone. My mother, visiting, had her wallet stolen on the bus; my wife lost two handbags in restaurants and suffered several incidents of groping on the subway. We had several break-ins at our country houses. One New Year's Eve, we stayed home and I went out to pickup Chinese food around 11:00 pm. It was very cold and windy, a bit of snow. The streets completely empty. Yet, I saw three different guys huddling or lurking in dark townhouse doorways in the course of a three block walk. New Year's Eve was an ideal night for muggings: drunk revelers carrying cash. I walked in the middle of the street.

One evening driving home down the FDR Drive, I was hit from behind, gently but firmly. The roads were icy and I was stopped behind another car. The bump from behind pushed me into the car in front. A frequent type of theft at the time in the New York area was to stage a minor automobile accident then, when the victim got out, to steal his or her car. Without thinking, I hopped out to inspect the cars. From the car behind me, five men quickly emerged. They were all well under six feet tall. I had on my cowboy boots, so I stood about 6'5". They promptly got back in their car and pulled around me and left. I tried to explain to the woman ahead of me that I had been pushed into her. She kept her windows closed, doors locked, and drove away. A thwarted car-jacking? Who knows?

The family moved to Georgetown for two years in 1993. It was quite a nice place to live, except for the crime. I understood that Georgetown had refused a Metro connection because it would increase crime. Well, even without a convenient escape route, we had five bicycles stolen from our garage in three separate break-ins. The strangest one was the theft of a pretty fancy trail bike my son had picked out for me for Father's Day at the neighborhood bike shop. The day after delivery, someone broke into the garage and stole it, still unused. When I called the shop for the registration number of the bike, I was told that they did not have it. Amazing. They had my address and the delivery date, but not the details of the expensive bike they had just sold.

I do think that the streets here have become more dangerous for me. I used to be cautious when I saw middle age women in big SUVs and old men. Recently, I have had some close encounters with a more diverse group of drivers. I hope it is not a growing trend.

Complicity

To keep informed, I reviewed recent studies of the involvement in slavery of two institutions with which I have been affiliated: the University of Cambridge, in England, and the Presbyterian Church in the U.S.A. Here are my observations.

Cambridge

In reaction to well-publicized events at American universities, Cambridge established a multidisciplinary Advisory Group to undertake an in depth investigation of the University's involvement with slavery and the slave trade (the Advisory Group on the Legacies of Enslavement).

"The scope of their research was to encompass both (a) historical (including archival) research into the ways in which the University may have been involved financially and otherwise in the slave trade or other historical forms of coerced labour connected to colonialism, and (b) the University's contribution to knowledge that may have supported the validation and dissemination of racialised and racist social structures and beliefs. Within their work, they were also asked to consider broader context, and especially the prominent place of Cambridge in the anti-slavery movement."

The report overview is now available (late summer 2022).

The Group acknowledges that:

"Cambridge University played an important role in the effort to end the slave trade and Caribbean slavery, and it is well-known that abolitionists pivotal to this movement, such as Thomas Clarkson, William Wilberforce, and Peter Peckard, once called Cambridge home. The abolition of the slave trade was one of the few issues that the City of Cambridge and University officials – racked by political, religious, and intellectual disagreements throughout the early modern period – had some degree of unity about. The University Senate sent petitions to the House of Commons in 1788 and again in 1792. Colleges, Masters, and Fellows also sent money to the Society for Effecting the Abolition of the Slave Trade.."

(Indeed, Clarkson performed a remarkable feat. "In 1785, Thomas Clarkson, a son of an Anglican clergyman in England, won an essay contest at Cambridge University with the prompt 'Is it right to make slaves of others against their will?' Clarkson ... had given little thought to the international slave trade and Black enslavement." William Yoo. *What Kind of Christianity*, p.53 (discussed below). His essay, published in 1786, debunked several the prevailing myths about the slave trade, for example, that most captives were prisoners of war, that the traders simply bought people that had already been enslaved by African kings, that European traders played a passive role as mere intermediaries and that the enslaved were largely docile and reconciled to their fate.)

The Group attempted to identify every benefit that the University derived from the existence of slavery, directly or indirectly, and every connection. But, the decision was made not to quantify them.

"While we consider financial connections in the form of donations and investment, the report also **tries not to make the research principally about numbers.** There can be no doubt that collectively the collegiate University gained economic benefit from colonial exploitation, which was itself based on the labour of enslaved people, as did the country as a whole, and the economic legacy of that gain has continued to the present day." (Emphasis added.)

They found the following:

1. Several alumni became slave owners. (A very small percentage.)
2. Some Colleges held stock or bonds in companies that participated in the slave trade. "Cambridge Colleges (those that have come to our attention being Corpus Christi, Gonville & Caius, Jesus, King's and Pembroke) directly purchased South Sea Company shares and annuities during the years of the company's major participation in the Atlantic Slave Trade." And, "East India bonds were owned by several Cambridge institutions, including Trinity College, although they do not seem to have reached the same extent as investments in the South Sea Company." (Likely, these investments constituted relatively modest amounts of the Colleges' wealth and of the companies' capital.)
3. The Colleges had many students who were the sons of slave holders and even actively recruited such sons. The Report says that the Colleges were "enriched" by the fees paid on behalf of those students. (The necessary implication is that the Colleges were in those days making a profit from the student fees over the costs of

educating the students; but, that is not explicitly stated and not demonstrated.)

4. Substantial gifts were received from benefactors who made some of their fortunes from slavery.

5. Some large gifts were received from benefactors whose wealth had largely derived from the slave trade or from slave labor. "In certain prominent cases donations came in the form of South Sea capital itself."

6. "As slavery and the slave trade came under scrutiny, some Cambridge intellectuals actively defended them while others passively accepted their continuation. ...Throughout the period under discussion individuals at Cambridge were writing about race, and presenting ideas that were used to justify the enslavement and colonisation of other people."

7. key institutions within Cambridge like the Fitzwilliam Museum memorialise those linked to slavery ... College benefactors ... whose wealth derived from slavery ... are memorialised in a variety of forms."

That is it.

The receipt of wealth directly connected to slavery seems to be the only one to single out criticism. All of the others are the "connections" that one would expect any institution of the size and prestige of Cambridge to have had. Indeed, most of us would be shocked or highly skeptical to be told that it had not. Moreover, many of us would question the wisdom or appropriateness of most conceivable actions or policies that would have attempted to prevent those connections. How would one control the future behavior of one's graduates? Do we want censureship of academic research? Of speech? Should one have attempted to monitor all the activities of any company in which one invested or all the sources of a benefactor's wealth (or tried to trace the sources of specific funds)? Would it have been right to refuse admission to a child based upon the business of the father? The Group made no such distinctions. Its recommendations are rather benign, but I think it should have issued a commendation rather than an indictment. But, in fact, the recommendations were probably inevitable as a minimum, even if nothing had been found.

I have no problem with a conclusion that certain gifts or bequests ought to have been turned down or returned, but I consider that to be a decision for the recipient to make. I have no objection to returning works of art to the country of origin if there are reasonable assurances that the works can be protected. Otherwise, I do not think that statues, portraits and building names can be said to "memorialize" the subject for more than a generation, maybe two. Thereafter, they become simply a reminder that we have a past or just a name. Finally, I think that the Group cast the net too broadly by including colonialism with slavery. There is an historical connection, of course, but colonialism had a separate existence and its own consequences, not all bad. For what it is worth, I rank the Opium Wars as the most disgraceful of British acts of the nineteenth century.

The Presbyterian Church

Here, I use a new book by theology professor William Yoo. He examines the relationship between the Presbyterian Church in America and slavery up to the Civil War. *What Kind of Christianity: A History of Slavery and Anti-Black Racism in the Presbyterian Church* (2022). (It now has the distinction of being the most expensive Kindle book that I have purchased. The two most expensive are also the two shortest, but the length is not relevant ebooks since the production cost is zero. Both books concern religion and race.)

The reviewers all praise Yoo for confronting or exposing the "complicity" of the Presbyterian Church in the U. S. With the existence of slavery in this country. Curiously, Yoo himself never explicitly asserts that the Church was "complicit", though he undoubtedly thinks so. He says, rather indirectly, that White Christians were complicit in Black slavery. For example:

- "..the need to identify and confront the sinfulness of white Christians in their active participation and **intentional complicity** in Black enslavement." *Id.*, p.28.
- "A plethora of white individuals and institutions in the northern states made moral compromises to accommodate enslavers and thusly **exhibit their complicity** in Black enslavement." *Id.*, p.173.

And, he quotes many others who made the accusation. *See, e.g.*, pp.36, 41. Not that this curious circumstance makes any real difference to my discussion below. I looked at the evidence he collected, not his conclusory characterizations.

Yoo's discussion of the official position of the denomination is relatively brief but scattered. Here are the basic points:

'In 1815, the PCUSA General Assembly commissioners affirmed an earlier resolution from **twenty years prior** that Black enslavement was a complicated matter requiring a charitable spirit of peace because of the great diversity of viewpoints within their denomination, but they **added to their resolution a note stating that the 'buying and selling of slaves by way of traffic' was 'inconsistent with the spirit of the gospel.'"**

"[T]he General Assembly in 1818 declared 'the **voluntary enslaving of one part of the human race by another**' was a 'gross violation' of human rights and **'totally irreconcilable with the spirit and principles of the gospel of Christ,** [but, the inclusion of] the exhortation to '**forbear harsh censures' toward enslavers i**n the same resolution resulted in **no concrete** actions toward Black liberation. ...[It] **denounced [slavery] in principle but recommended no disciplinary action against enslavers.**"

"In 1836, approximately 250 commissioners from across the northern and southern states gathered in Pittsburgh for the annual meeting of the General Assembly of the Presbyterian Church in the United States of America (PCUSA), the largest Presbyterian denomination in the nation with over 2,800 congregations and nearly 220,000 members. One of the matters these Presbyterians would grapple with was their church's position on the enslavement of more than two million Black persons."

Id., pp.13, 14, 49 (emphasis added).

But, You reports, "the 'subject of slavery' was introduced at one session with a majority report comprising a mere 211 words, postponed in two other sessions, and then indefinitely postponed by a vote of 154 in favor, 87 in opposition, and 4 abstentions." *Id.*, p.17. (Remember, the importation of slaves into the U.S. was suspended from the early 1770s until 1800, then banned in 1807, effective 1808. And, between 1774 and 1807, most northern states had banned slavery.)

In the end, his principal criticism of the official position is that it permitted slave owners to be Church members and to participate in the

Sacraments. He seems to believe that the only proper Christian thing to have done is banish them (and their families?) from the congregation and refuse them Communion, rather like some Catholics today think should be done to President Biden because of his advocacy of abortion. (Apparently, the Church had some 60,000 members in 1837 because they disavowed "original sin". *Id.*, p.184.) Was there a moral imperative to deny slave owners and supporters of slavery participation in the church community? Is that the Christian way? It certainly was not Christ's approach to sinners.

Yoo is obviously highly critical that Church leaders gave any weight to the facts that the future of slavery was a political matter, that it was very "complicated" or that there was widespread disagreement over what should be done. (And, all three were facts in the nineteenth century prior to the Civil War, especially with respect to what should happen to the people that had been enslaved.) Every one and all are to him irrelevant or only pretense. (Yoo notes that the two largest national denominational organizations both fell apart in the mid-nineteenth century (1857 for the new PCUSA and May 1861 for the original PCUSA), leaving just regional Presbyterian organizations until 1983. *Id.*, p.29. The splintering of the Church was largely due to disagreements related to slavery.)

Yoo identifies what he considers a falsehood about the Presbyterian Church and slavery, that people did not know the realities of slavery. If they were not fully informed, it was a conscious choice they made to be ignorant. Yet, Yoo's lengthy (and very informative and moving) summaries of a relative handful of largely autobiographical books published between 1836 and 1860 disclosing the truth about slavery belies his assertion. The information was not widely available, only the pamphleteering. Indeed, *Uncle Tom' Cabin* in 1851/1852 was met with charges of exaggeration, causing Harriet Beecher Stowe to publish a companion guide (a "Key") setting out evidence supporting her descriptions in 1853. *Id.*, pp.83-4.

And, of course, "normal conditions" were quite different then. Corporal punishment, including flogging, was commonplace in the nineteenth century. It was employed in schools, the military, the criminal justice system and in private homes. As another example, many immigrants had experienced very difficult trans-Atlantic crossings. Also, all the colonies had had indentured servitude, where the right to an individual's labor could be sold to another. *See* Note on Slavery, below. I do not mean to minimize the sufferings of slaves, but I think it creditable that many Americans did not appreciate the extent or severity of the abuses, attributing the worse incidents reported as the doings of a relative few "monsters".

As to the evidence of Church "complicity", Yoo cites the fact that many Presbyterians were slave holders, including several Presbyterian ministers; that there were reports that some Presbyterian slave holders engaged in physical abuse of slaves; and that many ministers preached biblical interpretations that portrayed slavery as God's will (the mark of Cain, the curse of Ham, various versions of Manifest Destiny). *See id.*, pp.189-95.

Certainly, there were many Presbyterian slave owners. Yoo cites estimates that 80,000 slaves were owned by Presbyterians in the 1850s, when Presbyterians numbered almost 400,000. But, Yoo estimates the number of Presbyterian slave owners as 50,000 to 75,000 in 1860 (averaging 1.1 to 1.6 slaves per owner?). *Id.*, pp.22-4. In the U. S. at the time, about 1.5% of the population owned slaves (averaging about 10 slaves per owner). Could it be that proportionally more Presbyterians owned slaves but far fewer than other groups? (No.) ** Yoo does not make that claim. Nor does he suggest that Presbyterians were more abusive than others. As for the biblical interpretations, absent evidence that they were advanced in bad faith, I fail to see that as immoral or complicit.***

So, we are left with the affirmative acts of individuals in their own lives. And, "guilty bystanders who chose to be complicit through inaction and indecision." *Id.*, p.29.

Perhaps, most striking to me is Yoo's reaction to what he perceives as greater attention being paid by many Presbyterians to the consequences of the rupturing of the denomination over slavery than to the consequences of slavery. He utilizes his strongest critical language in discussing that perceived error of priorities. For example,

> "I find it **deeply troubling** that the withering of Presbyterianism is attributed to these ecclesial schisms and not the active participation of white Presbyterians in slavery. It is also **infuriating** that Black enslavement is presented as a barrier to church unity rather than a tragedy. ... "[T]he **terrible result** is that some white Presbyterians today feel more **remorse** for church disunity than the oppressive abuse and reprehensible violence that their Presbyterian predecessors inflicted upon enslaved persons."

Id., p.30 (emphasis added).

And,

> "[O]ne struggles to find **the requisite anger** over the pain and torture that millions of enslaved persons suffered from white Presbyterian enslavers, supporters of Black enslavement, and **guilty bystanders who chose to be complicit through inaction and indecision.**"

Id., p.29 (emphasis added).

This obsession is odd. The state of the Church is clearly an appropriate concern of its members and is something that can be addressed currently. What about "Forgive and forget"?

"For I will forgive their iniquity,
and their sin I will remember no more."

Jeremiah 31:33-34

There is no doubt that after the Civil War, Presbyterians, like other white Americans, were strongly racist. The debates over what should be done with the freed slaves had focused on whether to send them back to Africa or to settle them in a new, separate territory in North America. (Since the vast preponderance of ex slaves had been born here and had no connections with Africa, the first option seemed cruel and highly coercive.) Few people then. thought full integration was desirable or even feasible.

I think that slavery presented levels of moral culpability. The most evil were the owners or masters who engaged in sexual or severe physical abuse of enslaved persons. The sins of these persons was not directly tied to slavery, but slavery dramatically opened up opportunities for persons inclined to sadism and violence. The next would be those who directly participated in and profited from the slave trade. The moral culpability of slave ownership, to me, depends upon how the ownership came about and how the owner thereafter behaved. But, the guilt of the "bystanders who chose to be complicit through inaction and indecision"?

Complicity by "indecision"?

An important part of the Reformation was that the church would no longer tell people what to think or do. People would be reasoned with, guided, persuaded, but look to their own conscience. I know that in the Reform tradition, there are differences in view as what the church should do to bring about social reform and a better world, but I am one who thinks that the Gospel emphasis is on the individual, on oneself and one's role as an example to others. We are not the judge and certainly not the enforcer (or executioner).

I do not intend to suggest that our Church history on this issue is something of which we should or could be proud or something that should be ignored. To the contrary, that history is something we should study and contemplate. Soberly. Not with anger or outrage nor condemn with sanctimonious rhetoric. (I suspect that the things that I find most objectionable about this book are the result of someone's efforts to make the book sell better, to attract more attention. That is unfortunate. There is a story that needs to be told. It should be told well.) We should strive to understand, to place ourselves in our predecessors shoes. Examine the positions taken and arguments made, on all sides of the issues, with empathy, not scorn, recognizing that the Presbyterian Church was and is made up of people, people with all of the human strengths and weaknesses, qualities both good and bad, the capacity for good and evil.

Remember, "let he who is without sin... " ("When they kept on questioning him, he straightened up and said to them, 'Let any one of you who is without sin be the first to throw a stone at her.'" *John* 8:7).

We can learn about ourselves from such an examination.

---

* We can do better. The U.S. Census data provides the best available information, and there was a census in 1860. The 1798 Census reported that slaves then represented about 18% of the population. Thereafter, even though the importation of slaves had been suspended since the 1770s and the slave trade banned in 1808, the slave population increased, but not as rapidly as the total population. By 1860, slaves constituted some 12.6% of the total. About 1.4% of the persons in the U. S. owned slaves, and about 7.4% of the families either owned slaves or used slave labor in their homes. In six Southern states, such family

percentages approached or exceeded 50%. So, we may assume that Yoo's data mixes up counting by persons with counting by families and that Presbyterians were pretty similar to the rest of the country. *See, e.g.,* Louis Jacobson, "Viral post gets it wrong about extent of slavery in 1860," *POLITIFACT,* August 24, 2017.

** To be "fair", Yoo does impugn the motives of the Church clergy, accusing them of being swayed by economic concerns, due in part to their very low pay. They allegedly tailored their messages to please members who owned slaves and to increase their chances of being called by larger, wealthier congregations. Those who owned slaves, often by marriage to wealthy women, were unwilling to give up through emancipation the wealth that the slaves represented. *Id.*, pp.223-32. However, he presents no evidence in support of his accusations, simply quoting similar unsupported accusations made in the nineteenth century. (And, he does not try to explain how so many men motivated by money world have chosen such a poorly paid profession.)

Further Notes on Slavery

Some books I have recently read include some interesting historical information about slavery in general.

From William Yoo, *What Kind of Christianity: A History of Slavery and Anti-Black Racism in the Presbyterian Church* (2022), I learned the fallowing:

The first sub-Saharan African taken to Europe as a slave was a woman seized by Portuguese slave traders in 1441. By the early 1500s, the Portuguese were transporting 3,000 enslaved Africans a year to Central and South America. The British participation began in 1563, with the capture and sale of 300 people from Sierra Leone to planters in the Dominican Republic. The demand for slave labor increased dramatically in the Caribbean as a result of the success of the plantations and the deaths of the indigenous slaves from imported diseases. That demand enticed European slave traders.

Between 1520 and 1630, England's population had more than doubled. The founding of Virginia was in part intended to help deal with the high numbers of poor and unemployed. The rapid popularity of the milder Virginia tobacco grown from Spanish seeds made tobacco the most profitable crop in the Southern colonies in the seventeen century. The demand for labor soared.

The primary source of that labor in Virginia was indentured servants, who contracted to work for a specified number of years in exchange for transportation to the New World and room and board for the duration, generally with little or no other compensation. There were plenty of takers in England.

"The... newcomers, more often than not, were indentured servants, allowing successful planters simultaneous access to land and labor, with no upfront cost to the company. Merchants and mariners reaped a benefit, too, for they recruited prospective servants, bargained their indenture terms with them, and then sold the contracts to planters in Virginia. ... **Approximately 50,000 servants—or three-quarters of all new arrivals—immigrated to the Chesapeake Bay colonies between 1630 and 1680.**"

Brendan Wolfe, "Indentured Servants in Colonial Virginia," *Encyclopedia Virginia,* October 2022 (emphasis added).

The first African slaves arrived in North America in 1619, only because the ship on which they were being transported to Mexico was seized by British privateers. Unfortunately, buyers were found. They were brought to Jamestown, Virginia, established as a fort in 1607, briefly abandoned in 1610, and becoming a town in 1619 (subsequently, the colonial capital). Some two-thirds of the initial settlors died in the first two years. (For context, the Mayflower landed in Massachusetts in October 1620. Half of the arrivals were dead by spring.)

African slave labor began replacing the European indentured servants and largely did so in the tobacco fields by the early eighteenth century.

The colonies did not then have laws regarding slavery, so the early arrangements were fluid. Many slaves were treated like indentured servants. And, slaves could be freed upon being baptized. In 1662, Virginia enacted a law providing that children of black mothers would have the status of the mother, not that of the white father. Other colonies followed, despite the long standing English tradition of patriarchy. Between 1664 and 1706, six colonies enacted laws declaring that Christian baptism would not result in emancipation, following the example of France. Finally, at the end of the eighteenth century, some of the newly-formed states enacted laws categorizing slaves as the personal property of the owners.

From David McCullough, *The Pioneers: The Heroic Story of the Settlers Who Brought the American Ideal West* (2022), I learned:

Ending the Revolutionary War, the Treaty of Paris of 1783 transferred from Britain to the new American country an enormous tract of contiguous land known as the Ohio country or Northwest Territory. This land, north and west of the Ohio River and extending to the Mississippi, had been "acquired" by the British from the French following the French and Indian War pursuant to the Treaty of Paris of 1763, and was devoid of European settlements.

In 1786-7, the U.S. Constitution did not yet exist, nor the Presidency. A private company was founded to propose the purchase and settlement of a part of the land across the Ohio River from Virginia (now West Virginia). The representative of the new Ohio Company, a Massachusetts pasror named Manasseh Cutler, approached the Continental Congress seeking a contract for the purchase of the land and the enactment of a law setting out a governance scheme for the Territory. The result was the Northwest Ordinance, enacted July 13, 1787.

The Ordinance provided that the Territory would be divided into between three and five states that would become part of the Confederacy, as it then was, and any successor sovereign entity. (Ultimately, the Territory became Ohio, Michigan, Indiana, Illinois and Wisconsin.) Remarkably, the Ordinance provided for freedom of religion, the promotion of public education, the protection of the property and lives of the indigenous peoples and the prohibition of slavery. (Excepts below.)

The protections for the Indians did not fair well after a confederation of 8 tribes attacked the settlors in 1790 and then defeated and decimated the forces of General St. Clair.

The next acquisition of land by the United States was the Louisiana Purchase in 1803. It posed quite different governance issues because the land was already populated by French and Spanish (largely Catholic and without a tradition of parliamentary government). There were also a sizable number of slaves, many recently brought by the Spanish who had continued the slave trade. The question of slavery was, thus, resolved on a state by state basis as new states were admitted to the Republic.

From the Northwest Ordinance

"Art. 1. No person, demeaning himself in a peaceable and orderly manner, shall ever be molested on account of his mode of worship or religious sentiments, in the said territory.

Art. 3. Religion, morality, and knowledge, being necessary to good government and the happiness of mankind, schools and the means of education shall forever be encouraged. The utmost good faith shall always be observed towards the Indians; their lands and property shall never be taken from them without their consent; and, in their property, rights, and liberty, they shall never be invaded or disturbed, unless in just and lawful wars authorized by Congress... .

Art. 4. The said territory, and the States which may be formed therein, shall forever remain a part of this Confederacy of the United States of America, subject to the Articles of Confederation, and to such alterations therein as shall be constitutionally made; and to all the acts and ordinances of the United States in Congress assembled, conformable thereto.

Art. 6. There shall be neither slavery nor involuntary servitude in the said territory, otherwise than in the punishment of crimes whereof the party shall have been duly convicted: Provided, always, That any person escaping into the same, from whom labor or service is lawfully claimed in any one of the original States, such fugitive may be lawfully reclaimed ... .

Done by the United States, in Congress assembled, the 13th day of July, in the year of our Lord 1787, and of their sovereignty and independence the twelfth."

WONDERING

I think that it is healthy for one to learn new things, to be exposed to diverse perspectives and interpretations. As a result, I have been reading a lot of books by people who see the world and its history differently than I am inclined to. But, I am learning. It is necessary to keep one's mind open and operating. That is much easier to do if the author one is reading has avoided politicizing the work and relied on evidence and reason. I am fully aware that everyone has biases and that any work of intellectual contribution will have a point of view. In fact, I am delighted when the author makes it explicit then moves on. I have already expressed my disagreements with some of the positions in some of these books, and I have made use of others. In those latter cases, I have often not agreed with everything said but found value and insight, nonetheless.

"Turn! Turn! Turn!"

"To everything (Turn! Turn! Turn!)
There is a season (Turn! Turn! Turn!)
And a time to every purpose,
under Heaven"

Pete Seeger
(1959)

The Byrds
(1965)

Although, I have now written about it several times, I find that my mind keeps wandering back to wonder what time really is. Carlo Rovelli declares: "The nature of time is perhaps the greatest remaining mystery." *The Order of Time* (2016), p.2. So it seems to me. I have written at length about all of the things we still do not understand about our world, but in most areas, one feels we are at least on the right trail to the answer. With respect to time, however, I feel we are just flailing. (Excuse the mixed metaphor.)

However, as Rovelli observes:

"We are not even clear about what it means 'to understand.' We see the world and we describe it: we give it an order. We know little of the actual relation between what we see of the world and the world itself. We know that we are myopic."

Id., p.210.

In 2017, I made limited use of Rovelli's book because he seemed too far from the main stream. Quantum gravitational theory, after all! But, I have gone back and reread it. Here is what I have concluded.

We can think of time as the process of aging. On our scale, everything ages; although, the relative "rate" of the aging will vary based on relative speed of travel and gravity. Aging consists of the conversion of mass to energy, energy to heat, dispersion of heat (from hot to cold) and the decrease in order (increase in disorder or entropy). Aging is a process that affects (or occurs in connection with) everything that is "ordered." Ordered things require the injection of energy to be maintained. The new energy combats the tendency to disorder. The system will not be in equilibrium.

There is no universal or absolute time. It is a purely local phenomenon, occurring or appearing in particular places. If, in the beginning, something is highly ordered (very low entropy), then the process of time is inevitable. "If we observe a phenomenon that begins in a state of lower entropy, it is clear why entropy increases—because in the process of reshuffling, everything becomes disordered." *Id.*, p.31. Otherwise, there is no time.

So, we say that our Universe necessarily began in a state of extremely low entropy, because time passes (and because time passes, there must have been a beginning). But, we come face to face with the question of why entropy was so low in the beginning. We are back to "The

Fine-tuning Problem," only with one more inexplicable condition, and a very big one. Our Universe **had** to be in a state of very low entropy in the beginning for us to exist now.

Rovelli tries to ameliorate this condition through the weak form of the Anthropic Principle. He postulates that it may be only in one or some parts of the Universe where time exists (a "subset"). In an infinite Universe with random configurations, there will be some configurations that just happen to have low entropy. *See id.*, pp.144-9. (Remember, anything that can happen does happen.) And, of course, for us to live, we must be in one of them. A Chinese science-fiction writer says:

> "The Creator gave the universe time. **Time not only brought change and progres**s, but also gave low-entropy entities existence. Time and the absolute-limit speed are two sides of the same blade that divided the universe, isolating most species of low-entropy entities and their civilizations **in tiny corners of the vast cosmos.**"

Baoshu, *The Redemption of Time* (2016), p.200 (emphasis added).

But, the causal relationship is likely reversed. Low-entropy spaces probably created time locally, not *vice versa*.

And, the low-entropy spaces? Just random events?

But, we have no evidence of and can imagine no experiment to test this hypothesis. And, in fact, it appears that entropy is increasing in the entire visible Universe. Indeed, Rovelli himself goes on to discuss time as if the whole Universe is involved.

We understand that at the level of elementary particles, things do not age. But, stuff happens. Things, or maybe just "fields", vibrate, move and change relationships with one another. Yet, there is no time.

"If I observe the microscopic state of things, then the difference between past and future vanishes. The future of the world, for instance,
is determined by its present state—though neither more nor less than
is the past. We often say that causes precede effects and yet, in the
elementary grammar of things, there is no distinction between 'cause'
and 'effect.'"

Rovelli, *The Order of Time*, pp.32-3.

So, if we were to observe at that scale, we would be unable to see "the
forest for the trees". From our vantage point, of course, we see only the
"forest", and we see the seasons change.

Therefore, does time only exist on our scale?

If so, is it, then, an emergent property of the macroscopic?

Although, Rovelli uses the word "emerge" frequently, he is not really
referring to "emergence", as I have discussed it elsewhere. He asserts that
the elements that constitute time exist everywhere, even though "time"
may not.

In a world without time, there must still be something that gives
rise to the time that we are accustomed to, with its order, with its past
that is different from the future, with its smooth flowing. Somehow,
our time must emerge around us, at least for us and at our scale.

Id., p.5.

Perhaps, then, the explanation is that time is observable only at a
certain scale or from certain perspectives, like the forest. It exists everywhere, but it can only be perceived in certain places. Rovelli stresses the
importance of point of view.

"If we give a description of the world that ignores point of view, that is solely "from the outside"—of space, of time, of a subject—we may be able to say many things but we lose certain crucial aspects of the world. Because the world that we have been given is the world seen from within it, not from without. Many things that we see in the world can be understood only if we take into account the role played by point of view. ...We must not, in short, confuse the temporal structures that belong to the world as "seen from the outside" with the aspects of the world that we observe and which depend on our being part of it, on our being situated within it."

Id., p.153.

Surely, in this he is correct.

But, he also tries to tie perspective into physical relationships (actually, interactions) and his theory of entropy. Those speculations, I do not buy. Rovelli cites well known thinkers who suggested that time was internal to mankind or not "real": Leibniz, Wittgenstein, Kant, Aristotle and St. Augustine. But, again, I think he is proposing something different.

"The entropy of the world in the far past appears very low to us. But this might not reflect the exact state of the world: **it might regard the subset of the world's variables with which we, as physical systems, have interacted.** ...[Perhaps] it wasn't the universe that was in a very particular configuration in the past. **Perhaps instead it is us, and our interactions with the universe, that are particular.** We are the ones who determine a particular macroscopic description. The initial low entropy of the universe, and hence the arrow of time, may be more down to us than to the universe itself. ...Perhaps, therefore, the flow of time is not a characteristic of the universe: **like the rotation of the heavens, it is due to the particular perspective that we have from our corner of it.**"

Id., pp.146-8, 150 (emphasis added).

In *Important Things*, I discussed three alternative interpretations of time: that it is an illusion, is a fundamental element of the Universe or is purely a human phenomenon. Seven years ago, I was inclined to the fundamental. But, now I perceive time as not fundamental, as used therein, but more as coincidental, to physics. Something that can happen. As to the perception of time, I see that as a phenomenon created by memory combined with consciousness. (Whether other animals have the requisite combination to experience time is an interesting question.) Past, present and future. What we live by. The past, with our memory; the future with our consciousness. The present? A bit complicated. To some extent, with our subconscious.

Yes, time may be a distinctly human phenomenon, arising from our particular position of observation. It is always there (at least, where entropy has not reached a maximum), but it is not always relevant. Except for us. It is embedded in, and integral to, the way our brains experience and relate to the world in terms of past, present and future. Without us to experience it, time would not exist.

"We inhabit time as fish live in water."

Id., p.1.

Origins (of Inequality)

Here, I turn again to the subject of inequality. From where or what and why did it emerge?

I start with the recent work of two U.K. anthropologists:

"Most of human history is irreparably lost to us. Our species, Homo sapiens, has existed for at least 200,000 years, but for most of that time we have next to no idea what was happening. ...[But,] evidence that has accumulated in archaeology, anthropology and kindred disciplines ... points towards **a completely new account of how human societies developed over roughly the last 30,000 years**. ...As we get to grips with the actual evidence, we always find that the realities of early human social life were far more complex, and a good deal more interesting, than any modern-day State of Nature theorist would ever be likely to guess."

David Graeber and David Wengrow, *The Dawn of Everything: A New History of Humanity* (2021), pp.1, 3-4, 15 (emphasis added).

The writings of modern "State of Nature theorists" that anthropologists Graeber and Wengrow criticizing are, specifically, Francis Fukuyama (*The Origins of Political Order: From Prehuman Times to the French Revolution*), Jared Diamond (*The World Until Yesterday:*

What Can We Learn from Traditional Societies?) and Steven Pinker (*The Better Angels of Our Nature: Why Violence Has Declined*).

Thomas Hobbes (1651) and Jean-Jacques Rousseau (1754) set forth depictions of the supposed "state of nature" (sharply contrasting ones reflecting opposing views of the inherent nature of man). But, neither purported to be presenting an historically accurate account of stone-age human existence. They were using their respective characterizations as analytical tools in the construction of political theories. The point Graeber and Wengrow seem to be making is that these subsequent theorists have tended to treat one or the other as an authoritative source about early mankind's social circumstances. (This charge seems unfair, certainly in connection with Fukuyama, whose book I have read.)

But, their real complaint is with the conclusions expressed about the evolution of human societies, especially with respect to the impacts of agriculture and population density. (They also challenge these writers' qualifications to opine on such a subject.)

Thus, they say:

> "[f]or Diamond and Fukuyama, as for Rousseau some centuries earlier, what put **an end to** that **equality – everywhere and foreve**r – was **the invention of agriculture**, and the higher population levels it sustained. Agriculture brought about a transition from 'bands' to 'tribes'. Accumulation of food surplus fed population growth, leading some 'tribes' to develop into ranked societies known as 'chiefdoms'."

Id., p.10 (emphasis added).

Graeber and Wengrow assert that the available evidence, much of it discovered in the last 50 years, presents something very different.

> "it is clear now that human societies before the advent of farming were **not confined to small, egalitarian bands.** ...**Agriculture, in turn, did not mean the inception of private property**, nor did it mark an irreversible step towards inequality. In fact, many of the first farming communities were relatively free of ranks and hierarchies. ...[A]surprising number of **the world's earliest cities were organized on robustly egalitarian lines**, with no need for authoritarian rulers, ambitious warrior-politicians, or even bossy administrators."

Id., p.4 (emphasis added).

In the body of their book, Graeber and Wengrow present evidence that the Paleolithic world was quite different than is commonly believed. There were much more diversity of social arrangements, there was a substantial amount of travel and regular social interactions among disparate groups, there were communal projects and "investment" in the future without centralized coercion and there were numerous centers of signifiant population. It also seems likely that most hunter-gather families consumed greater caloric intake with far, far fewer hours of labor than an English 19th century factory worker's family (enjoying, perhaps, as short a work week as a modem Frenchman). They also present examples of insightful critiques of Western "civilization" by indigenous inhabitants of the Americas, evidence of pre-civilization deliberations over political issues concerning the type of society in which people want to live and stories of how people exposed both to indigenous and Western living almost always opted for the former when they had the opportunity (*Dancing with Wolves* was not pure fantasy).

Indeed,

> "human remains from early agricultural societies do not attest to improved health or wealth but rather to deteriorating living standards as compared to those of hunter-gatherers living millennia before. Hunter-gatherers evidently lived longer, consumed a richer diet, worked less intensively and suffered fewer infectious diseases."

Oded Galor, *The Journey of Humanity: The Origins of Wealth and Inequality* (2022), p.30.

PRIVATE PROPERTY AND KINGDOMS

The anthropologists find early forms of private property and social/political hierarchy in connection with sacred objects and religious practices. Otherwise, however, they offer no explanation for the broad emergence of both.

The incidents of claims of personal possession would seem to arise out of relative scarcity. Things found in abundance are not likely to attract such claims. For example, the law of water rights developed quickly in the American West as the demand for water began to exceed the supply. Also, possessed things must be durable. So, a certain level of technology would seem necessary. It seems quite possible to me that someone created a useful object that required work or skill to make and asserted ownership of it. And, that that practice spread.

It is often said that the European settlors "stole" the land from the indigenous peoples, but that is not quite right. For the most part (the hunter-gathers), the original Americans did not consider the land to be owned by them. They had access, they used the resources, but did not purport to exclude others as such (although, tribes tended to have territories). The settlors, in contrast, assrted ownership of land and other resources, to the exclusion of others.

The right to exclude was the hallmark of European private property. Over time, the concept of property expanded to include a variety of rights. In American Constitutional law, both the due process clause and eminent domain reference "property". Do they protect contract rights, market value, the enjoyment of common goods? In modern jurisprudence, property is conceived as a bundle of rights (and some responsibilities). But, these rights require a legal system and some central authority.

Similarly, the presence of rulers seems tied to religious practices or warfare. It is not difficult to imagine how such a hierarchy would persist once established; but, why would a community submit to it in the first place?

One reason would be a crisis or external threat. One could assume that the emerging leader was perceived to offer something of value and then delivered. Again, little generalization from the many anecdotes.

So, the anthropologists fail to explain by generalizable processes the origins of private property, of capitalism (or feudalism), or of kingdoms, hierarchies or, even, social stratification. In the end, their examination of the archeological and anthropological evidence also fails to answer their fundamental question: Why is it that we have come to live in societies dominated by self-centeredness, greed, stress, insecurity and dramatic inequality, leaving so many isolated and lonely?

OUR CHOICE?

Actually, their central thesis, or argument, is that we today could and should choose to live a different sort of life, a different lifestyle, motivated by different values and goals. All in, however, I do not think they have made theat case.

First,

And, most importantly, their analysis fails to demonstrate that meaningful different alternative societies would be feasible in a world with billions of people.

They do not address the impact of the inevitable appearance of scarcity in early societies. Certain things that are possible in a world of abundance become much more difficult and unlikely when resources become scarce. So, "[t]he inability to sustain the growing population, as well as climatic changes, eventually induced humanity to explore an alternative mode of subsistence—agriculture." Galor, *The Journey of Humanity,*, p.20.

> "[T]he population size of agricultural societies stabilised at a new and higher level, but this time, in reverting to subsistence level, their living conditions actually became significantly lower than those of hunter-gatherers who had lived millennia before them, when existing ecological niches were not yet densely populated. Compared to the living standards of the hunter-gatherers who were their more immediate ancestors, however, the transition to agriculture was entirely rational, perhaps even inevitable; in fact, it did not reflect a deterioration."

Id., p.33.

And,

> "There were then in 1870 1.3 billion people alive, 2.6 times as many as there had been in 1500. Farm sizes were only two-fifths as large, on average, as they had been in 1500, canceling out the overwhelming bulk of technological improvement, as far as typical human living standards were concerned."

J. Bradford DeLong, *Slouching Towards Utopia: An Economic History of the Twentieth Century* (2022), p.16.[1]

The fact is that if everyone concluded that we wanted to live like the American Plains Indians, it is simply not possible for us all to do so. Some very few of us, yes; but, only if the rest disappeared.

Second,

Inequality of wealth requires wealth, which means there must be both a surplus over subsistence and the existence of things that can store value.

> "It is apparent ... that neither surpluses nor shortages prevailed indefinitely during the Malthusian epoch. The introduction of novel crops or technologies magnified the rate of population growth, mitigating their impact on economic prosperity, while the long-term economic devastation of ecological disasters was ultimately averted by their adverse effects on population via famine, disease and wars."

Galor, *The Journey of Humanity,* p.39.

"[B]ack in the preindustrial Agrarian Age, technological progress led to little visible change over one or even several lifetimes, and little growth in typical living standards even over centuries or millennia." DeLong, *Slouching Towards Utopia,* p.14.

So, what we need to know is what forms of society have the capability to escape the Malthusian trap of population growth denying anything beyond mere subsistence level poverty in the long run.

The only one we can safely identify is the capitalist market economy that banished Malthus after 1870. "Things changed starting around 1870. Then we got the institutions for organization and research and the technologies—we got full globalization, the industrial research laboratory, and the modern corporation. These were the keys. These unlocked the gate that had previously kept humanity in dire poverty." *Id.,* p.2.

Why, then, did the capitalist market economy succeed?

"[Friederich August von] Hayek observed, the market economy crowdsources—incentivizes and coordinates at the grassroots—solutions to the problems it sets. ... All societies ... face **profound difficulties in getting reliable information to the deciders and then incentivizing the deciders to act for the public good.** The market order of property, contract, and exchange can—if property rights are handled properly—push decision-making out to the decentralized periphery where the reliable information already exists, solving the information problem. And by rewarding those who bring resources to valuable uses, it automatically solves the incentivization problem."

Id., pp.2, 93 (emphasis added).

How many of today's societal "ills" are inherent in or crucial to that economic success? Market-based capitalism clearly implies inequality, because it depends on there being winners and losers. It is facilitated by arbitrage, so windfalls are an integral part of the system. The prospect of gain and the threat of losses power the system, providing the incentives to do things better. Trade itself involves inequality as the result and covetousness as the impetus. The benefits of division of labor, specialization, economies of scale, comparative advantage, decentralized decision-making and rapid transmission of relevant information result in economic growth. Private ownership of the means of production and of natural resources brings the discipline of the marketplace to the allocation and utilization of assets and capital. "In a market economy, the good cause that justifies inequality is that we need to incentivize economic growth by rewarding skill, industry, and foresight, even if doing so inevitably involves rewarding good luck as well." *Id.*, p.415.

Third,

They fail to establish that people today would choose their proffered alternative even if it were practical or feasible.

There have been a multitude of popular demands for reform and change, and many of them have been successful. But, only for modifications in the system, not radical transformation. For example, in 1896, the U. S. middle rejected the radical Democrats and elected McKinley as President. In 1848, the French peasantry rejected reforms that would have assisted the urban poor. *See* DeLong, *Slouching Towards Utopia*, pp.100-03 ("It was not so much that crucial swing voters ... swung to the Republican side. It was, rather, a huge countermobilization against William Jennings Bryan and a turnout increase that determined the outcome of the election"), 106-09 ("the farmers of Tocqueville's France sided against the socialists").

Even today, the protesters do not generally advocate a change in the underlying system, but rather a reallocation of the sysem's abundant output. The key differences in political views are about what will kill the goose that lays the golden eggs. The dispute is whether the wealthy are the gift that can keep giving. Most people will continue to assess the size of their slice of the pie and not be pleased with a larger percentage of a smaller pie if it a smaller piece.

> "[The] rights that society will attempt to validate do not —or might not—be rights to anything like an equal distribution of the fruits of industry and agriculture. And it is **probably wrong to describe them as fair: they are what people expect,** given a certain social order. **Equals should be treated equally, yes; but unequals should be treated unequally.** And **societies do not have to and almost never do presume that people are of equal significance."**
>
> ...
>
> "Perhaps there was, at bottom, a near-innate human aversion to even semicentralized redistributive arrangements that take from some and give to others. We do not always want to be the receiver: it makes us feel small and inadequate. We do not always want to be the giver: that makes us feel exploited and grifted. And as a matter of principle and practice, we tend to disapprove whenever we spy a situation in which somebody else seems to be following a life strategy of always being the receiver."

Id., pp.96, 414 (emphasis added).

The fact is that most people are not much bothered by inequality as such. They are much more focused on their own standard of living and how it compares to that of their neighbors. This is not like the feudal world where the land holdings of a few nobles deprived the masses of plots of their own. Land reform had the potential to increase the size of the total pie, while also altering its allocation. I see no current proposals for redistribution that have that potential. Instead, many well-off individuals highlight the apparently growing inequality as a means of achieving political power, an historic reason for the fomenting class warfare.

I am not arguing in favor of any particular level of inequality. Perhaps, it is too great today. But, as I previously wrote, I have seen no good evidence or even arguments to that effect. However, I have elsewhere set out my proposals for the rationalization of the U. S. Federal tax system. Implementation of those proposals would reduce inequality. However, I propose them not as a redistribution scheme, but as a commonsensical, rational approach to taxation, one that is in the interests of the country.

WEALTH OF NATIONS

Why were the benefits of capitalism so unevenly shared among countries? (I touched on this question in the essay "Unequality" in *The Eyes Have It*.) "[T]he immense disparities in the wealth of nations are rooted in a chain of causal factors: at the surface are proximate factors, such as the technological and educational differences between countries; at the core are the deeper and ultimate factors – institutions, culture, geography and population diversity – that lie at the root of it all. Galor, *The Journey of Humanity,* p.142. "While in industrial nations the gains from trade were directed primarily towards investment in education and led to growth in income per capita, a greater portion of the gains from trade in non-industrial nations were channelled towards increased fertility and population growth." *Id.,* p.137.

The economic historians identify a few important differences among nations that contributed to the different economic results. I present some composite quotations.

Education/Human capital

- "[I]n the centuries leading up to industrialisation, as Europe started to make strides in technology and trade, the importance of education began to intensify. During the subsequent phases of the Industrial Revolution, the demand for skilled labour in the growing industrial sector markedly increased. From here on, and for the first time in history, human capital formation – factors that influence worker productivity, such as education, training, skills and health – was designed and undertaken with the primary purpose of satisfying the increasing requirements of industrialisation for literacy and numeracy as well as mechanical skills among the workforce."

- "... [O]ther civilisations that had previously outpaced Europe in technological development, including the Chinese and the Ottoman, had started to lag behind.... . This technological divergence was reflected in a widening literacy gap between Europe and the rest of the world. ... In non-European societies, however, literacy rates started to rise only in the twentieth century."

- "...[I]nvesting in the education and the skills of the workforce became increasingly more important to the capitalist class, not less so, as they came to realise that of all the capital at their disposal, it was human capital that held the key to preventing a decline in their profit margins."

Galor, *The Journey of Humanity*, pp. 64, 67, 64, 65, 74.

- "The United States made the creation of a literate, numerate citizenry a high priority. And that encouraged those with richer backgrounds, better preparations, and quicker or better-trained minds to go on to ever-higher education."

DeLong, *Slouching Towards Utopia*, p.77.

Government

- "One short and too-simple answer is that the fault lies with governments—specifically, with governmental institutions that were 'extractive' rather than 'developmental,' ... . We are talking here about kleptocracy: rule by thieves."

- "Most governments at most times in most places have followed policies that show little interest in nurturing sustained increases in productivity. ...Only after the government's seat is secure will debates about development policy take place. But the pursuit of a secure hold on power almost always takes up all the rulers' time, energy, and resources."

- "Through misfortune and bad government, India and China had failed to escape the shackles of the Malthusian Devil [until the second half of the twentieth century]."[2]

- "Reza Shah Pahlavi's answer was to try to turn Iranians into Europeans—that is, to follow an authoritarian state-led development road reminiscent of pre–World War I Imperial Germany. But this left scant place for Islam. And the state that resulted was highly corrupt. ...In January 1979 Reza Shah Pahlavi fled into exile. Thereafter, Iran's economy stagnated."

- "Those countries where the armies of Stalin or Mao or Kim Il-Sung or Ho Chi Minh or (shudder) Pol Pot had marched were, on average, only one-fifth as well-off when 1990 came and the curtains were raised as those that had been just beyond those armies' reach."[3]

- "Successful economic development depends on a strong but limited government. Strong in the sense that its judgments of property rights are obeyed, that its functionaries obey instructions from the center, and that the infrastructure it pays for is built. And limited in the sense that it can do relatively little to help or hurt individual enterprises, and that political power does not become the only effective road to wealth and status. ...Only a state that is limited in the amount of damage it can do to the economy, or a state that is secure enough, independent enough, and committed enough to rapid economic growth, can avoid these political survival traps."

DeLong, *Slouching Towards Utopia*, pp.349, 350, 44, 352.

- Generally, "good" (supportive of development) government cannot be created overnight. Indeed, it can take hundreds of years of tradition. The same with a pro-development culture.[4]

- The exceptions seem to be South Korea and several Southeast Asian Pacific Rim countries that embraced the model of Japan-- export led growth stimulated by currency and trade policies that made imports expensive and exports very competitive. That strategy could not work for everyone since it required other countries that were avid consumers willing to bear trade deficits. (Not every country can have a positive balance of payment at one time.) For these countries, the United States was their savior.[5]

Redistribution Policies/Consumption

- "One can imagine an alternative scenario in which European governments maintained and expanded wartime controls in order to guard against substantial shifts in income distribution. In such a case, the late 1940s and early 1950s might have seen the creation in Western Europe of allocative bureaucracies to ration scarce foreign exchange ...[or take other steps] to protect the living standards of the urban working classes—as happened in various countries of Latin America, which nearly stagnated in the two decades after World War II. ...Yet Europe avoided these traps. ...Western Europe's mixed economies built substantial systems for redistribution. But they built these systems on top of—and not as replacements for—market allocations of consumer and producer goods and the factors of production."

- "Argentina's leaders responded to the social and economic upheavals by adopting new policies aimed at stimulating demand and redistributing wealth. At the same time, Argentina's leaders became ... more inclined to use controls instead of prices as mechanisms to allocate goods. ...Post–World War II Argentina saw foreign exchange allocated by the central government in order to, first, keep existing factories running and, second, keep home consumption high."

- "In Latin America, an overvalued exchange rate would see a lot of society's wealth spent on the purchase of foreign luxuries, as the upper class preferred to live well rather than channel its resources... ."

DeLong, *Slouching Towards Utopia*, pp.317, 352, 354, 366-7.

The balance between things that promote growth and those that retard it seems to be rather delicate. It is hard to know what changes will make a difference. And, experimentation is difficult because it can take years to see the consequences, by which time corrective action may be difficult. Indeed, much depends upon the attitudes/expectations of the people. It is psychological, which can be very difficult to alter. Take inflation. Once everyone believes that inflation is inevitable, it is inevitable. The discipline of the market breaks down.

Of course, the market deals largely with property and money, so it best serves those who have both. As DeLong asserts:

> "A market economy can only produce good results if it defines the general welfare appropriately—if it weights the material well-being and utility of each individual in an appropriate manner as it adds up and makes tradeoffs. And the problem is that the value that a market economy gives an individual depends on his or her wealth."
> *Id.*, p.332.

It has been less successful with labor, since labor is harder to unitize than capital or natural resources. Labor is not easily standardized or measured. What is the unit? So, we have persons receiving stupendous economic rents and others not being paid enough to live independently. DeLong observes, "Depending on which aspect of income distribution was highlighted, either industrial capitalism produced an income distribution that was too unequal (rich get richer, the rest stay poor) or not unequal enough (respected lower middle classes slip into joining the unskilled proletariat)." *Id.*, p.265.

And, of course, no one has figured out how to create a functioning market solution for other human needs.

[1.] I was quite impressed with this book, despite its length. DeLong actually presents fairly conflicting ideas. Writing primarily as an historian, he provides insight after insight. I am not knowledgeable enough to recognize which are original and which are borrowed, but I learned a lot. Although, he pays lip service to the liberal talking points (excess inequality, too much priority given to money and property, too little promotion of other rights), his analytical skills keep pushing his prejudices to the periphery, a problem his intellectual hero Paul Krugman certainly does not have.

[2.] "The failure of the British Raj to transform India poses an enormous problem for all of us economists. Under the British Raj in the late nineteenth and early twentieth centuries India had a remarkable degree of internal and external peace, a tolerable administration of justice, and easy taxes. Yet no sign of progress 'to the highest degree of opulence' had occurred." DeLong, *Slouching Towards Utopia*, p.120.

[3.] "[With the] government by Park Chung-Hee in 1961, everything changed. Park was brutal (although not extraordinarily so by the standards of the twentieth century) but remarkably effective. The shift of Korea's development strategy from one of import substitution to one of export-led industrialization was very rapid. The consequences were astounding." DeLong, *Slouching Towards Utopia*, p.369.

[4.] "[In Japan, t]here followed the rapid adoption of Western organization: prefects, bureaucratic jobs, newspapers, language standardization on Tokyo samurai dialect, an education ministry, compulsory school attendance, military conscription, railways built by the government, the abolition of internal customs barriers to a national market, fixed-length hours of the working day to improve coordination, and the Gregorian calendar, all in place by 1873. Representative local government was in place by 1879. A bicameral parliament (with a newly created peerage) and a constitutional monarchy were in place by 1889. By 1890, 80 percent of school-age children were at least enrolled." DeLong, *Slouching Towards Utopia*, p.133.

5. "East Asia started with the assumption that it would have to export—and export big-time—if only because its resources were thin and scarce. ...Japan then provided a model for how its ex-colonies, South Korea and Taiwan, should attempt to play catch-up under their dictators (Park Chung-Hee and Chiang Kai-shek, respectively), which then provided models for Malaysia, Thailand, and others. ...First, trade, but managed trade. Undervalue the exchange rate.... . Very patient cheap capital helped. ...Add a high rate of savings... . Tilt the economy's price structure so that machines that embodied modern technological knowledge were cheap and foreign-made and luxurious consumption goods were expensive. ...Taking these steps would mean, of course, heavy, hidden taxes on labor, and especially on skilled labor." DeLong, *Slouching Towards Utopia*, pp.365, 366, 367.

Beauty and Truth

George McDonald
Thomas Wingfold, Curate

Since the beginning of the Scientific Revolution, many scientists have believed that one characteristic of a good or true scientific theory was elegance or beauty. Admittedly, a bit elusive to define, but something we would know when we see it. Initially, that belief presumably had theological roots, expectations about God's design of the World, but it has lived on with no explanatory basis, other than faith based on experience. Rationally, this belief should be found mainly among those who demand understanding from science, not satisfied with mere accuracy of predictions; but I have detected no such correlation.

Of course, a subjective or human-based criterion like beauty seems odd in the context of science. There have been attempts to define beauty and even to make it quantifiable. Obviously, it must be more than simplicity, which, like Occam's Razor, is inherently relative. Twentieth-century scientists have talked of "rigidity", meaning that the whole theory collapses if one removes a piece of it. That does not suggest "beauty" to me, however. Another term used is "naturalness", referring to the absence of contrived or "fine-tuned" elements or parameters. That is better, but incomplete.

A scientist turned writer, Sabine Hossenfelder, wrote a book a few years ago purporting to show that physicists' preoccupation or obsession with beauty was hampering scientific advancement, *Lost in Math: How Beauty Leads Physics Astray*.

"Mathematical rigidity I had to discard because it rests on the selection of *a priori* truths, a choice that is itself not rigid, turning the idea into an absurdity. Neither could I find a mathematical basis for simplicity, naturalness, or elegance, each of which in the end brought back subjective, human values. In using these criteria, I fear, we overstep the limits of science."

Sabine Hossenfelder, *Lost in Math: How Beauty Leads Physics Astray* (2018), p.94.

Her principal example, from her own experience, is the continuing pursuit of certain proposed theoretical additions to particle physics despite some 30 years of empirical failures because they would be beautiful and elegant if true. However, she is unable to propose any ugly theory that has been ignored yet could do the job. She similarly fails to provide evidence that those toiling away so far in vain could have been more productively employed. Finally, she does not argue, or substantiate the argument, that a useful theory is likely to be rejected if it is ugly.* But, she does ponder this intriguing philosophical question: "I already know that the world embodies beautiful ideas. I want to know whether the world embodies ugly ideas, and if so, **whether we would continue to think of them as ugly.**" *Id.*, p.145 (emphasis added).

Perhaps, truth is beauty, but is it necessarily beautiful? Do we see truth as beauty?

In the modern view, beauty is relative, culturally determined. In fact, we are suppose to believe that all value systems are relative and, perhaps, equal. So, what about truth? Is truth culturally determined? Is one person's truth as good as any other's? Well, our concept of truth is certainly homocentric. It is culturally influenced. Yet, we resist.

Her other examples tend to fall into the realm of cosmology, where it is normal for a handful of empirical observations to support a vast theoretical structure. "Again we see that it's a reliance on mathematics together with a desire for simplicity that leads to multiple universes." *Id.*, p.104. So, string theory, inflation, dark matter, dark energy and multiple universes. The proponents of those theories say: "It's not us; it's the math that made us do it. And math doesn't lie. We are merely being objective, good scientists, they say. If you're opposing these insights, you are in denial and just refuse to accept inconvenient logical consequences." *Id.*102.

Yes,
but...

"...[B]are facts about how the physical world works ...
are both powerful and strangely beautiful, to be sure.
But the style of thought that allowed us to discover them
is a great achievement, too."

Frank Wilczek, *Fundamentals* (2022), p.xi

Yet, the problem with the multiple universe and similar is not that the theorists favored beauty over truth. It is that they ignore the scientific standard of empirical falsifiability. Indeed, they even dispense with empirical confirmability. It seems to suffice to be able to say "nothing proves me wrong". The danger is the loss of what Frank Wilczek referred to as "the style of thought that allowed us to discover" the facts of nature—the scientific method. Of course, again, scientific progress has arisen, and can continue to arise, from the investigation of speculative hypotheses. And, it often takes much time and many false starts. Also, the devising of empirical test can require time, ingenuity and skill.

And, then there is the question of the reality of truth. Is there such a thing as truth? If so, can we ever find it? Or, will it always be receding just out of our reach? Is truth like an elusive idea? Like a dream that is always vaniching?

"'Evanescent as a rainbow... . It is a thing that was known, but, from the moment consciousness turned its lantern upon it, began to become invisible. ... [I]t seems only to be turning corner after corner to evade the mind's eye, but behind every corner it leaves a portion of itself; until at length ... it is gone so utterly that the mind remains aghast in the perplexity of the doubt whether ever there was a thought there at all."

George McDonald, *Thomas Wingfold, Curate* (1880).

The question of "what is reality" is difficult. It is hard to know whether one should look to philosophers, neuroscientists, physicists or cosmologists for the answer.

Speaking of cosmologists, they bring us a new possibility—that the Universe is a 3D hologram. *See* Dennis Overbye, "Black Holes May Hide a Mind-Bending Secret About Our Universe: Take gravity, add quantum mechanics, stir. What do you get? Just maybe, a holographic cosmos", *NYT.com*, October 12, 2022 (emphasis added).:

> "[I]n 1997 ... Juan Maldacena, a theorist at the Institute for Advanced Study in Princeton, N.J., used new ideas from string theory ... to create a mathematical model of the entire universe as a hologram. In his formulation, **all the information about what happens inside some volume of space is encoded as quantum fields on the surface of the region's boundary.** ... Galaxies, black holes, gravity, stars and the rest, including us, are ... inside, and the information describing them resides on the outside... ."

Now, how about that? Beautiful?

---

* I have been critical of this book, but my dissatisfaction is entirely with the theme identified in the title, which I assume was selected in the belief that it would sell books (if you do not have sex or an attack on religion, a criticism of mathematical science may be the next best thing). The preponderance of the book itself is an excellent discussion of the Standard Model of Particle Physics and possible revisions to it. The best I have read.

FOR FELLOW
TRAVELERS

Some Tips

Advice for my caregivers that others might find useful.

The BiPap mask

- To put on, fit the mask firmly under the nose, centered and level. If too high, it blocks my nostrils. If too low, there will be a high leak. Then, while holding the mask in place, pull the straps over my head.
- If the mask is crooked on my face, it is usually because the straps are misplaced.
- If the mask is leaking around my cheeks, try tightening the strap on the side opposite the leak.
- To remove the mask, lift the straps from the back. Then pull the mask forward off the face.
- For suctioning, hold the top of the mask in place under my nose and lift the bottom to uncover my mouth. Put the tip straight in the center of my mouth.
- I generally need to tilt back enough to raise my head for the suctioning to work effectively. Otherwise, my throat can be obstructed.

The lift

- When going up, I need my hands on my knees to support myself.
- Before lifting, be sure that my fingers are not caught in a towel or blanket or the sling, since they cannot stand my weight.

- Once I am lifted, if my hands slip, it is not possible to put them back.
- When coming down, make sure that my toes are not curled under when they reach the footrest.
- If the lift and chair are not lined up, you can move the lift even if I am in it. It has wheels.

Feet

- When I could no longer stand or walk, my feet became badly swollen, resulting in nerve damage. As a result, my toes are very sensitive to the touch. Light touch is the worst, causing a burning sensation. A firm touch hurts but is bearable.
- Due to muscle deterioration from ALS, the tops of my feet and my ankles are pretty painful when pressed, but I need to keep the circulation going.

Drinking

- It is necessary to tip the cup or glass to let the liquid flow into my mouth, but then I need to lower my chin in order to swallow.

Wheelchair

- I need to tilt back pretty far in order to breathe comfortably and to hold my head up. Sometimes I need a push forward to let my spine straighten up or to align my bottom, lower back, shoulders and head with each other.
- When pushing or pulling me forward, do so from my shoulders so I bend from the waist. Not from the back of my neck, which mainly compresses my chest.
- When helping to move my hands, check to be sure my elbows are on the armrests.

About The Author

Diagnosed with ALS in 2015 and confined to a wheelchair in 2018, he wrote his first collection of essays, entitled *Wanderings of a Captive Mind*. A second set of essays, *The Eyes Have It* (Wanderings Part 2), was written entirely using his eyes. Those essays are by practical necessity shorter and without the many references. This new set, also written primarily with his eyes, is Part 3 of Wanderings. Born in Columbus, Ohio, and raised in Northville, Michigan, John majored in economics at Amherst College (Class of 1970) and received his J.D. from The Harvard Law School in 1973. Following law school, he did post-graduate research at the University of Cambridge (Trinity College). In late 1974, John began a 37-year career as a commercial litigator with a major law firm in New York City. John retired from the practice of law in 2011 and, shortly thereafter, located just outside of Cambridge, England. In March 2015, however, after his diagnosis, he returned to the U.S., settling in Old Town Alexandria, Virginia. His daughter Sarah and his son John Eliot and daughter-in-law Megan, with his two grandchildren, Hannah and Jeffrey, all live nearby.

www.ingramcontent.com/pod-product-compliance
Lightning Source LLC
Chambersburg PA
CBHW071524150726
48000CB00002B/667